ANY BODY IN A CROCKPOT!

MIXING RECIPES WITH DEVOTIONS

SLOW COOKING YOUR WAY TO HEAVEN

Illustrations by
Chelsea Marietta Moore

First Printing - March 2009
Copyright © 2009

ISBN Number:
978-0-9744972-4-2

Library of Congress Control Number:
2009902714

Printing in the United States of America

Stephens Printing, LLC
642 Hwy 469 South
Florence, MS 39073
stephensprint@yahoo.com

BLONDETRODUCTION

Hi! I'm Debbie. I am A.D.D. and I'm BLONDE. I want to 'temper' you through my other 3 books before I 'whip' out **Any Body Can Cook In A Crockpot! Slow Cooking Your Way To Heaven**.

Any Blonde Can Cook! was written mostly from family recipes and because I am so A.D.D. I needed a step by step form to follow without getting distracted. I also had to have big, bold over 45 print because I am at that age. I needed a little humor so I sprinkled blonde jokes in for some more flavor.

Any Blondette Can Do It! originally was Any Blonde Can Do It! and I started wondering, "Am I really a blonde?" I added a brunette to the cover because a blondette is a cross between a blonde and a brunette. You see, you don't have to be blonde to have ANOTHER BLONDE MOMENT.

How To Meat A Blonde Brunette or Redhead! is my favorite of the three because whenever I cook a recipe it revolves around which meat I am cooking. So this cookbook is broken up into sections by Beef, Chicken, Pork, Seafood and Wild Game. Each meat section has sides for a complete meal.

Which brings me to, **Any Body Can Cook In A Crockpot! Slow Cooking Your Way To Heaven**. It still has the easy, step by step format, with the big, bold now over 50 print. Now instead of the blonde jokes the cookbook has scripture with my Blonde A.D.D. interpretation of what each scripture means to me. I interpreted it in rhymes so I really had to have my blonde thinking cap on. I left spaces if you want to fill in the blanks about what each scripture means to you. You can use it as a cookbook or as a biblical study guide with recipes.

For 47 years I lived my life with no purpose, besides living for myself. But God put our family in a new neighborhood, and a house across the street from a Baptist preacher and his family with an unbelievable spirit for the Lord.

You see, I began writing these cookbooks for myself and my own glory. Since it has been about five years ago these cookbooks are somewhat a testimonial analogy of the changes in my life. Now He has shown me how humor in the kitchen and in daily living can season your life, especially if you add in belief, scripture and a spirit that seeks God.

Don't get the idea this is some professor discussing the Bible. I'm still blonde and you may find your interpretation of scripture is different than mine. You might call it "food" for thought.

This cookbook also mixes in easy crockpot recipes which will allow you to cook something different in your crockpot while you're working, running errands, watching TV or serving others in some way.

My wish is you will peel away anything in your life that He brings to your heart. Whip it out of your life. Stew in His word. So you can be whisked away in His love.

WHAT ARE THOSE THINGS ON THE COVER?

Come right on in my Crockpot and meet my Angel Elves. These were real and mainly my sin. Each Elf (and I call them Angel Elves because they made me who I am today) represented my shallowness. I know you are thinking those are flat out devils. At one time they felt like devils and if I hadn't changed they would be devils. Now they are my Angel Elves.

They describe my life. I allowed these elves to dilute my spiritual **Strength, Concentration, Quality** and **Purity**.

My **Strength** was my appearance. That was **Plastic Peggy**. She thought if she looked better on the outside she would feel better on the inside. She was soooo self-sufficient. It was all about her. She didn't use her Crockpot she used her Microwave.

My **Concentration** was temporary, fleshly and based on earthly things. I focused on what I could buy and not on having eternal peace. That was **Diamond Debbie** and **Shopping Sherry**. Instead of cooking, she went out to eat. She was looking to buy fulfillment. She wanted to be Served.

My **Quality** was fruitless. My faithfulness was serving my own needs. That was **Tongue-lashing Terry**. She didn't have love, joy, peace, patience, kindness, goodness, faithfulness, gentleness or self-control. She was Broiled. She was done on the outside but raw on the inside.

My **Purity** was a corrupt heart. **Whino Wanda** didn't percolate her wine. She didn't filter anything. She lived externally rather than an Internal reality.

I know this is really **Blonde** but each one of these elves was part of me. I was dying in those roots for 47 years. I hope this Cookbook makes cooking easier. And, I hope you find the peace and joy I found in applying these principles to my life.

Read the Recipe. (**HIS word**)

Cover the bowl with slow cooker bags. (**Prayer**)

Leave the lid on while cooking. (**Trust HIM**)

Toss the slow cooker bag. (**Confess**)

Serve a fabulous meal. (**SERVE others**)

4

Sticks & Stones Can Break Bones..
And Words Can Hurt!

I used to say things without thinking, not understanding the repercussions. Words can KILL someone's spirit. Words can send you into Depression. Words can MURDER. Words can make someone think they are WORTHLESS. That is what my words did to most people in my life and especially to my son.

I guess I didn't really understand the consequences of words because it wasn't a substance. But words hurt, just as alcohol numbs your pain temporarily. Or immorality punishes the ones you love. Or lies make you feel better about yourself.

Imagine living with someone who called you a loser all of the time. Or someone who went crazy when you couldn't see things her way. Or someone who blames you for everything. Or someone making you feel like you are always wrong.

That someone was me. I am a verbal and emotional abuser. I can't think of anyone close to me that I didn't tongue-lash.

My life has always been full of turmoil. That was just my personality and I was just going to have to live with it. I went to church, I prayed, I read the Bible, sometimes. I never thought I was smart enough to understand the Bible so I relied on someone else to explain it by reading their devotions and their interpretation.

After going through a divorce, raising two children and building a successful company, I looked at my life and I was 47 years old and nothing was better. Children. Money. Clothes. Cars. Houses. Success. None of these made me feel better inside. I had so much guilt and pain but I never connected it to my verbal abuse. I just thought that was me. That was the personality God gave me.

I didn't think I had a real problem. It was not until I started writing this testimony that I realized that was my sin. My tongue. Oh, I knew my tongue was sharp. I knew my tongue had hurt many people, but I wasn't drinking or doing drugs. Those were real addictions. I wasn't an addict.

I just needed something different in my life. I played around in a relationship with God for many years but it wasn't until my tongue again was used to hurt someone that I cried out to God to help me get rid of all of my pain.

I remember the moment I was confronted, I felt anger. Well, I will show her. Then I wanted to just move away. How dare she confront me?

Instead, I prayed and asked God to guide me, to take over my life. Still not knowing until this very moment what my real pain was. He was in the process of changing my heart because of my obedience in reading His word and the steps I was taking in having a real relationship with Him. I was trying to change something that I had never admitted.

You see when I became a Real Believer, a Real Christian at 47 my life didn't change immediately. It has been a gradual process. I thought when I asked God to come into my life that I was doing Him a favor. I was helping him get more people into His kingdom, just what I had read He wanted from us.

Now, I know why I couldn't understand this. I was reading God's word but I hadn't turned it all over to Him. I had invited Him in but I still was living in the flesh. Satan still had hold of me and was allowing me to think this was just the way I was.

Because of my obedience to God in the past two years he allowed me to UNDERSTAND His word and LISTEN to Him and HEAR Him.

This has been the most pain I have ever felt because it is embarrassing and some of you may never understand. God does have a sense of humor because he has allowed me to write my story in a cookbook of all places.

No, God didn't sprinkle his dust and, poof, make me understand. I had to get to know Him and tell Him and listen to Him and love Him.

He just led me day by day. Now, with God's love, the pain is easing. Sometimes it even disappears, replaced with the peace of knowing of His unfaltering love for me, flaws and all, and his promise of eternal life.

BLONDICATION

This is the part that doesn't mean anything to anybody except me. It took many loving, caring people in my life to get me where God wanted me to be.

To **My Heavenly Father,** for sending His Son to forgive me of my sins so I could mess up nineteen hundred thousand times. Knowing He has forgiven me and loves me no matter what kind of mess I make.

To my husband, **Terry** who put up with me when I couldn't even stand being around myself. For 15 years he accepted all of my blondeness.

To my son **Dakota**, who I wish I could have a do-over with because all of the hateful, mean words I called him when he was just a child. I am so proud of what he has accomplished in his short time.

To my daughter **Chelsea**, who accepted God's calling at an early age because she didn't have a Mother capable of providing what she needed. She also tested recipes, co-authored How To Meat A Blonde, Brunette or Redhead! and illustrated this cookbook.

To my **Father**, who provides love and who washes all of my dishes after I cook recipes for the cookbooks. I am so proud of how he has grown in his personal relationship with God.

To my **Mother**, who loved me when I wasn't loveable. To her husband, **Richard** for marrying her so I wouldn't have to take care of her. (Just Kidding).

To my friend **Christy,** who was there whenever I was crying out for help. She was able to show me what God's true love looks like. She is the Author of **Heart, Mind and Soul** in this cookbook. How appropriate since she was so patient in helping me find my Heart, Mind and Soul.

To her husband, **Chip** and their children, **Rachel, McKenzie, Regan** who accepts all of my faults and still loves me.

To **Peggy,** My best friend for 30 years who would come over and eat chicken when I was poor and single. She listened to my blonde stories without making me feel dumb. She cried with me through many heart-aches. She laughed at my blonde moments. She has always been there whenever I needed her and I love her so much.

To **Angel**, who was the greatest 11 year old stand in Mother for Dakota and Chelsea. She loved them when I wasn't able to love anyone. She was one of the few that really understood me.

To **Anne Marie**, who I feel God sprinkled into my life to show me how I act and to show me the Fruit of the Spirit, her Mother gave her. That is why she was the only one I wanted to write about the **Fruit of the Spirit**.

To her husband **Chris**, who listened to the last 48 years of my life and didn't judge me. I felt he genuinely loves me for who I am. To their children, **Darby** and **Molly** for loving Debbie Blonde.

To **Amy**, who prayed many prayers for my pain and healing. She was the only one I felt God wanted to write about **Sin** because she accepts hers just as she accepts mine.

To **Ginger**, who wrote about **Prayer** and **Reading the Bible**, while her Mother was in the emergency room. God called her and she was obedient.

To **Karen**, my first Precept teacher and **Melissa**, my Precept leader right now and to everyone in both those classes that prayed for me. **Aimee** where are you? **Kelly**, thanks for helping with the back of the book and for being YOU.

To **Cynthia**, who would take my blonde A.D.D. mumble jumble and make me feel like it was the best writing in the world and say, "I didn't have to change much." HA! She accepted my thoughts in Blondenese and gave me the encouragement, in my lack of confidence head, to feel like my writings weren't too bad.

To **Karen**, Stephens Printing backbone, who corrected change after change for this cookbook. (Can you imagine the changes an unsure, A.D.D. Blonde has?)

To the **1,600 store owners or buyers**, that bought my other cookbooks and products, allowing me to continue writing cookbooks. **Rose**, thanks for listening to me when I didn't think I could make it. **Mark**, thanks for the scriptures.

Vicki, Mr. & Mrs. Caldwell, for embracing my poor spirit.

Weekly Menu Planner

DAY _____   _____   _____

Meats _____p___ _____p___ _____p___

Sides _____p___ _____p___ _____p___

Extra _____p___ _____p___ _____p___

What I will Need ...	Have/Need	Whatever else I need...
_____	☐ ☐	_____
_____	☐ ☐	_____
_____	☐ ☐	_____
_____	☐ ☐	_____
_____	☐ ☐	_____
_____	☐ ☐	_____
_____	☐ ☐	_____
_____	☐ ☐	_____
_____	☐ ☐	_____
_____	☐ ☐	_____
_____	☐ ☐	_____
_____	☐ ☐	_____
_____	☐ ☐	_____
_____	☐ ☐	_____
_____	☐ ☐	_____
_____	☐ ☐	_____
_____	☐ ☐	_____
_____	☐ ☐	_____
_____	☐ ☐	_____
_____	☐ ☐	_____
_____	☐ ☐	_____
_____	☐ ☐	_____
_____	☐ ☐	_____
_____	☐ ☐	_____
_____	☐ ☐	_____

How To Use Menu Planner

DAY **Monday**   **Tuesday**   **Thursday**

Meats **Cranberry Brisket** p 113   **Green Chilies Stuffed Chicken** 169   **Roasted Pepper Tenderloin** p 201

Sides **Potato Salad** p 97   **Salad** p___   **Corn Pudding** p 85

Extra _____ p___   _____ p___   _____ p___

What I will Need ...	Have	Need	Whatever else I need...
(2-3 lb) beef brisket	☐	☑	lettuce
whole cranberry sauce	☑	☐	tomatoes
8oz tomato sauce	☑	☐	foil
onion	☑	☐	feta cheese
mustard	☐	☑	toilet paper
potatoes	☑	☐	paper cups
celery	☐	☑	chocolate chips
bell pepper (1)	☑	☐	sandwich meat
balsamic vinegar	☑	☐	bread
parsley	☐	☑	creamer
bacon	☐	☑	washing powder
cream cheese	☑	☐	spray n wash
cheddar cheese (Sh)	☑	☐	water
green chilies	☑	☐	diet cokes
chicken breasts (4)	☐	☑	mascara
cream mushroom soup	☑	☐	
hot enchilada sauce	☐	☑	
pork loin (3 lb)	☐	☑	
dry ranch dressing	☑	☐	
sour cream	☐	☑	
roasted peppers	☐	☑	
eggs	☑	☐	
milk	☑	☐	
bag frozen corn	☐	☑	
	☐	☐	

APPETIZERS

'create in me a
clean heart,
O, God.

HEART & MIND

create in me a
clean heart,
O, God.

Heart, Mind & Soul

There is a treasure that has been placed within each human being, a treasure that sets us apart from every other part of creation. Within all of us, there lies a heart, a mind and a soul.

Our heart is not only an anatomically life-sustaining organ, but also the center of our emotions and total personality. The mind is the element of our being that reasons, thinks, feels, wills, perceives and judges.

Our soul is the principle of our existence that is completely eternal and is the very seat of our moral feelings and sentiments. Every other portion of this universe will pass away, yet our souls will live forever.

I have chosen to believe that we were created in the image of an eternal God who loves us unconditionally. He has, since the beginning of time, desired that his people would completely give themselves back to Him... heart, mind and soul.

Not only do we have a heart, mind and soul, but we also have been given the capacity to choose who or what we will devote ourselves to in our time here on earth. We naturally have a tendency towards selfish desires, and the pursuit of anything other than this is a result of consciously choosing to do so.

Our time here is limited, and it definitely passes rapidly. Even if we live to be 100, this lifetime is a vapor compared to eternity. Therefore, I am coming to understand more and more the urgency of cultivating a healthy heart, mind and soul.

By God's perfect design all three are tightly woven together. A combination of what we feel emotionally, what we know intellectually and what we believe morally creates the essence of who we are as individuals. God desires that we choose to give back to Him this beautiful treasure that He has given to us, and in doing so we literally give to Him ourselves, completely and undivided.

From the time I was a little girl, I began learning stories about God and retaining information about spiritual things. My mind was filled with potentially life-changing truths. As a young teenager, I begin to sense God moving in my life. I was coming to realize that these truths that I had locked in my mind were intended to change my heart. God tenderly drew me unto Himself through other believers and the truth of His Word. Not only did my belief encompass my mind, but I was learning to embrace these truths with my heart, as well.

Salvation was God's free gift to me. Christ was crucified so that the sin debt of the world would be cancelled. When Jesus was resurrected, death was conquered and a brand new hope entered into the world. He made possible the transformation of my empty, sinful, broken life into a fulfilling, forgiven, restored life. The hope of Heaven remains my source of strength in a wicked, deteriorating world.

I understand that while I remain here in the flesh, temptations will always be present in my life and I will still, at times, give in to these temptations but, there is no negative circumstance that I cannot flee or endure with the help and power of the resurrected Christ. This is something I believe with all of my mind and all of my heart.

My soul now rejoices. It rejoices because I have an eternal purpose. I remain on this journey, all along the way seeking how the Father may be glorified in my life.

I am healthiest physically, emotionally and spiritually when I love and serve those less fortunate. The revealed purpose of my life is to glorify God and to share His saving love and grace with others. In order to maintain a healthy relationship with God, it is imperative that I ask Him to renew my mind and fill my heart with His overwhelming power daily...He is faithful.

Christy Henderson

12

Au jus

To serve with natural juices or gravy; Not to be confused with au choo, a sneeze.

Bake

To cook by dry heat in an oven; Not to be confused with lying out in the sun.

Artichoke Dip
"Dip, Don't Choke In The Prophets"

3	(6 ounce) jars marinated artichoke hearts
1	cup mayonnaise
1	(2 ounce) jar diced pimientos
1	cup shredded Parmesan cheese
1	cup sour cream
¼	teaspoon garlic powder

COMBINE all ingredients in crockpot. MIX well.
COVER.COOK on LOW for 2 hours or HIGH for 1 hour.
SERVE with crackers.

Bacon Cheese Dip
"Cheesy Ones Choose To Dip"

16	turkey bacon slices, cooked, crumbled
2	(8 ounce) cream cheese, cubed
4	cups shredded cheddar cheese
1	cup half and half cream
2	teaspoons Worcestershire
1	teaspoon dried minced onion
½	teaspoon dry mustard
½	teaspoon salt
	hot sauce, to taste

COMBINE all ingredients in crockpot. MIX well.
COVER. COOK on LOW for 2 hours or HIGH for 1 hour.
SERVE with crackers.

create in me a
clean heart,
O, God.

SLOW

He said to them, How foolish you are, and how slow of heart to believe all that the prophets have spoken.
Luke 24:25 (NIV)

BLONDE A.D.D. INTERPRETATION:

I'M TELLING YOU HOW TO BELONG DON'T LET IT TAKE SO LONG

YOUR INTERPRETATION:

____ ____ ____ ____ ____ ____

____ ____ ____ ____ ____

create in me a clean heart, O, God.

Bean Beef Dip
"Beef Up Those Lips Not To Dip"

1½	pounds lean ground beef, browned, drained
1	(14 ounce) can diced tomatoes
1	envelope dry onion soup mix
¼	teaspoon pepper
2	teaspoons chili powder
¼	cup ketchup
¼	teaspoon garlic powder
¼	teaspoon dried basil
½	red onion, chopped
2	(14 ounce) cans kidney beans, with liquid

COMBINE all ingredients in crockpot. MIX well.
COVER. COOK on LOW for 3 hours or HIGH for 1½ hours.
SERVE with chips.

Refried Bean Dip
"Bean Re-Fried From The Lips"

2	(20 ounce) cans refried beans
½	teaspoon salt
2	cups shredded cheddar cheese
1	(4 ounce) can diced green chilies
½	cup taco sauce
½	cup green onions, chopped

COMBINE all ingredients in crockpot. MIX well.
COVER. COOK on LOW for 2 hours or HIGH for 1 hour.
SERVE with chips.

create in me a clean heart, O, God.

MOUTH

The Lord says: These people come near to me with their mouth and honor me with their lips, but their hearts are far from me. Their worship of me is made up only of rules taught by men. Isaiah 29:13 (NIV)

BLONDE A.D.D. INTERPRETATION:

YOUR HEART NOT YOUR WORDS WILL MAKE YOUR LIPS HEARD

YOUR INTERPRETATION:

_____ _____ _____ _____ _____

_____ _____ _____ _____

create in me a
clean heart,
O, God.

Chili Beef Dip
"Chill & HE Will Show You HIS Will"

3	cans chili beef soup
1	(8 ounce) cream cheese, cubed
1	cup sour cream
2	Tablespoons water
2	teaspoons prepared mustard
2	teaspoons Worcestershire
1	teaspoon chili sauce
½	teaspoon hot pepper sauce

COMBINE all ingredients in crockpot. MIX well.
COVER. COOK on LOW for 2 hours or HIGH for 1 hour.
SERVE with chips.

Cream Cheese Beef Dip
"Dip For The Cream Of HIS Word"

2	pounds lean ground beef, browned, drained
1	onion, chopped
1	jalapeno pepper, seeded
2	garlic cloves, crushed
1	(4 ounce) can diced green chilies
1	teaspoon salt
2	(8 ounce) cans tomato sauce
½	cup ketchup
1	teaspoon oregano
2	(8 ounce) cream cheese, cubed
½	cup shredded Parmesan cheese
1½	teaspoons chili powder

COMBINE all ingredients in crockpot. MIX well.
COVER. COOK on LOW for 3 hours or HIGH for 1½ hours.

"create in me a clean heart, O, God.

MIND

Then he opened their minds so they could understand the scriptures.
Luke 24:45 (NIV)

BLONDE A.D.D. INTERPRETATION:

YOUR HEART AND MIND WILL HELP YOU FIND

YOUR INTERPRETATION:

_____ _____ _____ _____

_____ _____ _____ _____

Italian Beef Dip
"Beef Up Your Heart & Mind"

1½	pounds lean ground beef, browned, drained
1	cup shredded Mozzarella cheese
1	envelope dry spaghetti sauce mix
2	(15 ounce) cans tomato sauce
3	cups shredded sharp cheddar cheese
2	Tablespoons cornstarch
½	cup dry red wine
	French bread, cut in chunks

COMBINE 1st 5 ingredients in crockpot. MIX well.
COVER.COOK on LOW for 3 hours or HIGH for 1½ hours.
DISSOLVE cornstarch in wine.
POUR cornstarch/wine mixture in crockpot. STIR.
COVER. COOK on HIGH for 15 minutes.
SERVE with French bread or crackers.

Salsa Beef Dip
"Any Heart & Mind Can Salsa"

1½	pounds lean ground beef, browned, drained
1	pound process cheese spread, cubed
1	(15 ounce) can cream-style corn
1	(12 ounce) jar chunky salsa

COMBINE all ingredients in crockpot. MIX well.
COVER.COOK on LOW for 3 hours or HIGH for 1½ hours.
SERVE with chips.

create in me a
clean heart,
O, God.

TEST

Test me, O LORD, and try me, examine my heart and my mind.
Psalms 26:2 (NIV)

BLONDE A.D.D. INTERPRETATION:

YOU PASS HIS TEST
YOU WILL BE BLESSED

YOUR INTERPRETATION:

_____   _____   _____   _____

_____   _____   _____   _____

create in me a
clean heart,
O, God.

Swiss Corned Beef Dip
"A Swiss Family Of Understanding"

1	(8 ounce) bottle Thousand Island dressing
4	cups shredded Swiss cheese
3	(2 ounce) packages corned beef, chopped
1	(16 ounce) can sauerkraut, drained

COMBINE all ingredients in crockpot. MIX well.
COVER.COOK on LOW for 2 hours or HIGH for 1 hour.
SERVE with crackers.

Mexican Broccoli Cheese Dip
"Dipping From The Mexican Heart"

1	(16 ounce) frozen chopped broccoli, cooked, drained
1	(8 ounce) Mexican process cheese spread, cubed
1	(8 ounce) process cheese spread, cubed
2	cans cream of mushroom soup
$\frac{1}{2}$	cup sour cream
1	Tablespoon garlic salt

COMBINE all ingredients in crockpot. MIX well.
COVER. COOK on LOW for 2 hours or HIGH for 1 hour.
SERVE with vegetables, chips or crackers.

TRUST

Trust in the LORD with all your heart and lean not on your own understanding.
Proverbs 3:5 (NIV)

BLONDE A.D.D. INTERPRETATION:

WHEN YOU THINK YOU MUST IT'S HIM YOU CAN TRUST

YOUR INTERPRETATION:

____ ____ ____ ____ ____

____ ____ ____ ____ ____

create in me a clean heart, O, God.

Green Chilies Cheese Dip
"My Heart Was Chili"

2	Tablespoons flour
2	eggs, beaten
1	(12 ounce) can evaporated milk
4	(4 ounce) cans diced green chilies
3	cups shredded Monterey Jack cheese
3	cups shredded cheddar cheese
1	(8 ounce) can tomato sauce

COMBINE 1st 3 ingredients in a bowl.
SPRAY crockpot with cooking spray.
LAYER ½ flour mixture, ½ chilies, ½ cheeses in order given.
REPEAT. COVER. COOK on LOW for 7 hours.
POUR tomato sauce on top when mixture is done.
COOK on HIGH for 15 minutes. SERVE with chips.

Picante Taco Cheese Dip
"My Heart Is Dipping"

1	2 pound process cheese spread, cubed
1½	pounds lean ground beef
⅔	cup water
1	dry package taco seasoning mix
1	(16 ounce) jar picante sauce

MELT cheese in crockpot on HIGH until cheese melts.
BROWN beef in skillet. DRAIN. ADD next 2 ingredients.
STIR beef mixture in crockpot with melted cheese.
ADD salsa. STIR. COOK on HIGH for 45 minutes.
SERVE with chips.

www.anotherblondemoment.com

"create in me a clean heart, O, God.

ACTIONS

The heart is deceitful above all things and beyond cure. Who can understand it?
Jeremiah 17:9 (NIV)

BLONDE A.D.D. INTERPRETATION:

GOD WEIGHS YOUR HEART AND ACTIONS DON'T LET MAN BE A DISTRACTION

YOUR INTERPRETATION:

_____ _____ _____ _____ _____

_____ _____ _____ _____ _____

create in me a clean heart, O, God.

Cajun Crab Dip
"I'm Not Crabby With My New Heart"

6	green onions, chopped
1	bell pepper, chopped
2	Tablespoons margarine
4	cups shredded process cheese
2	cups Monterey Jack cheese, cubed
1	(10 ounce) can diced green chillies & tomatoes
	garlic powder, to taste
	hot sauce, to taste
	salt & pepper, to taste
1	pound fresh crabmeat or 3 (6 ounce) cans

SAUTE' 1st 3 ingredients in a skillet. **PUT** in crockpot.
ADD next 7 ingredients in crockpot. **MIX** well.
COVER. STIR. COOK on **HIGH** until cheeses melt.
ADD crabmeat. **COOK** on **LOW** for 1 hour.
SERVE with crackers.

Crabmeat Cheese Dip
"Dip Your Heart"

4	cups shredded process cheese
1	cup sour cream
1	(8 ounce) cream cheese, softened
1	(4 ounce) can sliced mushrooms, drained
3	(6 ounce) cans crabmeat

COMBINE 1st 3 ingredients in crockpot. **COVER.**
COOK on **HIGH** until cheeses melt. **STIR.**
ADD last 2 ingredients. **STIR.**
COOK on **LOW** for 1 hour or **HIGH** for 30 minutes.
SERVE with crackers or chips.

create in me a
clean heart,
O, God.

COVENANT

This is the covenant that I will make with the house of Israel after that time, declares the LORD. I will put my law in their minds and write it on their hearts. I will be their God, and they will be my people.
Jeremiah 31:33 (NIV)

BLONDE A.D.D. INTERPRETATION:

GOD GAVE US A NEW COVENANT
HIS BLESSING OF SALVATION IS EVIDENT

YOUR INTERPRETATION:

_____ _____ _____ _____ _____

_____ _____ _____ _____ _____

'create in me a clean heart, O, God.

Wine Crab Dip
"Don't Whine & Be Crabby"

2	(8 ounce) cream cheese, cubed
1	cup mayonnaise
½	cup sour cream
2	teaspoons garlic salt
½	cup white wine
1	Tablespoon dry sherry
3	green onions, chopped
3	(6 ounce) cans crabmeat

COMBINE 1st 7 ingredients in crockpot. **COVER.**
COOK on **LOW** for 2 hours or **HIGH** for 1 hour.
STIR. ADD crabmeat. STIR.
COOK on **LOW** for 30 minutes or **HIGH** for 15 minutes.
SERVE with crackers or chips.

Crawfish Sausage Dip
"Don't Crawfish My Heart"

1	pound sausage
½	cup onion, chopped
½	cup bell pepper, chopped
2	Tablespoons garlic powder
1	can cream of mushroom soup
1	pound Mexican process cheese spread, cubed
2	teaspoons Creole seasoning
2	pounds fresh crawfish or frozen

BROWN 1st 3 ingredients in a skillet. **DRAIN.**
COMBINE sausage mixture with next 4 ingredients in crockpot.
ADD crawfish. STIR. COOK on **HIGH** for 1 hour.
SERVE with crackers.

www.anotherblondemoment.com

'create in me a
clean heart,
O, God.

HEART

I will give you a new heart and put a new spirit in you; I will remove from you your heart of stone and give you a heart of flesh.
Ezekiel 36:26 (NIV)

BLONDE A.D.D. INTERPRETATION:

YOUR NEW HEART IS PLIABLE AND WILL RESPOND
YOUR HEART WON'T BE SELF-WILLED AND BLONDE

YOUR INTERPRETATION:

___ ___ ___ ___ ___ ___ ___ ___ ___

___ ___ ___ ___ ___ ___ ___ ___ ___

"create in me a
clean heart,
O, God.

Grape Jelly Meatballs
"Make It Click To Stick"

1   (32 ounce) bag frozen meatballs, thawed
1   (14 ounce) bottle ketchup
1   (12 ounce) bottle chili sauce
1   (10 ounce) jar grape jelly

PLACE all ingredients in crockpot. STIR.
COVER. COOK on LOW for 4 hours or HIGH for 2 hours.

Ranch Mushrooms
"Mushy & Room For The Lord"

2   (8 ounce) fresh whole mushrooms, washed
1   stick margarine, melted
2   envelopes dry ranch dressing mix

COMBINE all ingredients in crockpot. MIX well.
COVER. COOK on LOW for 4 hours or HIGH for 2 hours.

Pizza Dip
"Dipping For God's Dust"

2   (8 ounce) cream cheese, softened
1   (8 ounce) jar pizza sauce
1   (4 ounce) can chopped black olives
$\frac{1}{2}$ cup onion, chopped
1   (3 ounce) sliced pepperonis
2   cups shredded pizza cheese

SPREAD cream cheese in bottom of crockpot.
COMBINE next 4 ingredients in a separate bowl.
SPREAD pizza sauce mixture over cream cheese.
SPRINKLE with cheese.
COOK on LOW for 2 hours or HIGH for 1 hour.
SERVE with crackers.

www.anotherblondemoment.com

create in me a clean heart, O, God.

REJOICE

Then Hannah prayed and said: My heart rejoices in the LORD; in the LORD my horn is lifted high. My mouth boasts over my enemies, for I delight in your deliverance.
1 Samuel 2:1 (NIV)

BLONDE A.D.D. INTERPRETATION:

MY HEART IS SO VERY HAPPY THAT I HAVE A RIGHTEOUS PAPPY

YOUR INTERPRETATION:

_____ _____ _____ _____ _____ _____ _____

_____ _____ _____ _____ _____

create in me a clean heart, O, God.

Shrimp Dip
"Submitting Shrimp"

2	turkey bacon slices
1	onion, chopped
12	shrimp, raw, peeled, chopped
1	tomato, chopped
3	cups shredded Monterey Jack cheese
4	drops hot sauce
⅛	teaspoon cayenne pepper

COOK bacon in skillet until crisp. **DRAIN. CRUMBLE.**
SAUTE' onions in bacon drippings until soft. **DRAIN.**
COMBINE all ingredients in crockpot. **COVER.**
COOK on **LOW** for 1 hour. (**THIN** with milk if too thick.)
SERVE with chips.

Spinach Dip
"Strengthening Spinach"

2	(8 ounce) cream cheese, cubed
½	cup whipping cream
1	(16 ounce) frozen chopped spinach, thawed, drained
1	(2 ounce) jar diced pimientos
2	teaspoons Worcestershire
½	teaspoon garlic salt
1	cup shredded Parmesan cheese
½	teaspoon thyme

COMBINE all ingredients in crockpot. **MIX** well.
COVER. COOK on **LOW** for 3 hours or **HIGH** for 1½ hours.
SERVE with vegetables, crackers or bread.

create in me a
clean heart,
O, God.

OBEDIENCE

Love the Lord your God with all your heart and with all your soul and with all your mind and with all your strength.
Mark 12:30 (NIV)

BLONDE A.D.D. INTERPRETATION:

GIVE IT TO HIM AND DO HIS WILL
LOVE HIM SERVE HIM AND HE WILL FULFILL

YOUR INTERPRETATION:

____ ____ ____ ____ ____ ____ ____ ____ ____

____ ____ ____ ____ ____ ____ ____ ____

create in me a
clean heart,
O, God.

Chex Mix
"No More Mixed Heart"

2	cups wheat Chex cereal
2	cups corn Chex cereal
2	cups rice Chex cereal
3	cups thin pretzel sticks
1	(13 ounce) can salted peanuts
1	teaspoon garlic salt
1	teaspoon celery salt
½	teaspoon seasoned salt
2	Tablespoons grated Parmesan cheese
⅓	cup margarine, melted
⅓	cup Worcestershire

COMBINE 1st 9 ingredients in large paper bag.
EMPTY chex mixture in large bowl.
POUR remaining 2 ingredients over Chex mixture.
TOSS gently with hands.
POUR Chex mixture in crockpot. COVER.
COOK on LOW for 4 hours or HIGH for 2 hours.
TEAR open bag. SPREAD Chex mixture on bag.
LET dry for 1 hour so bag will absorb moisture.

Baking Sheet

A good baking sheet (also known as a cookie sheet) are thick and the best ones are insulated; Not to be confused with a insulated mat you lay on while laying in the sun.

create in me a
clean heart,
O, God.

SEARCH YOUR HEART

I the LORD search the heart and examine the mind, to reward a man according to his conduct, according to what his deeds deserve.
Jeremiah 17:10 (NIV)

I am working on my heart not having any deceit
As I study GOD'S word my life is becoming complete.

I know in my heart, mind and soul how to live a fulfilled life
Before I chose this way to live, my life was full of strife.

My life is not perfect by any stretch of the imagination
But now I have help, I live on the Rock, HIS foundation.

Rising every morning with journaling and prayer
Reading GOD'S word, helps me prepare.

For what is coming to me that very day
When I get off track I just speak to HIM and pray.

This is all for you, don't let me think it is about me
Talking to HIM about everything is the key.

My heart is being changed because my obedience in HIS word
Meditating and studying allows HIS words to become heard.

The people that knew me before this transformation
Won't believe I wrote this, she has no concentration.

They would be correct it wasn't me that was able to do this
The completion of this book shows HE really does exist.

SOUPS

"I have everything, but I'm still not satisfied."

SIN

Sin

"I have everything, but I'm still not satisfied."

There are many different forms and types of Crockpots. There are many different forms and types of Sin. A Crockpot is a Crockpot. Sin is Sin.

My life is like a Crockpot in the fact that it is a container. I was created to be a container for God's purpose and enjoyment. God wants to be delighted and enjoy what my Crockpot creates. A Crockpot has controls set to cook what has been placed in its container which will eventually supply a fabulous meal. I have also been taught not to lift the lid while cooking in a Crockpot.

What controls are my Crockpot set on? Are my controls: greed, selfishness, envy, anger, meanness, and unwillingness to help others? These are all forms of Sin that every age group, no matter how young or old, fights each day. My controls should be properly set on love for God and others, patience, kindness, self-control and always willing to help others.

Think about how things turn out if you set the controls the wrong way. For example, a roast when cold forms a thick layer of grease. When red beans are cooked too long, they are mushy. If bisque is cooked too fast at a high temperature, it forms a gross, dark ring around the top. None of these are appetizing. They are not enjoyable.

Sin is the same way in God's eyes. Sin causes greasy layers to build up, mush and become hard and dark. I must make sure my controls are set on the proper settings each day.

What is my Crockpot plugged into? It has to be plugged in to receive power. Do I plug in to the path of Sin each day or do I plug into God? Do I plug in to what is acceptable in the world's eyes or what is pleasing to God's eyes?

These are questions that I ask myself each day. Just because I am following Christ does not mean sin vanishes. Sin is a battle that every human being deals with every day all day. Sin is Sin. Is what my Crockpot's set on and plugged in to going to help me fight Sin?

Thank God for His grace and mercy. God provided the way to rid ALL Crockpots of Sin. His name is Jesus Christ. He is the most awesome ingredient added to a recipe that is pleasing to God. By the shedding of His blood, we are saved. Our Crockpots are clean. The grease, the mush and the dark ring have been washed white as snow. John 3:15-16

No matter our age, our dress size or the color of our hair, we should try each day to set our controls correctly, get plugged in to God's WORD and keep the lid on.

Amy Murray

SOUPS

"I have everything, but I'm still not satisfied."

SIN

Asparagus Soup
"Oh Spare Us The Tongue"

2   pounds fresh asparagus, cut in 1 inch pieces
3   (14 ounce) cans chicken broth
4   green onions, chopped
2   large potatoes, cubed
           salt & pepper, to taste

COMBINE all ingredients in crockpot. COVER.
COOK on LOW for 6 hours or HIGH for 3 hours.

Broccoli Soup
"HIS Tongue Makes You Young"

2   cans cream of celery soup
1   (18 ounce) jar Cheez-Whiz
1   pint half and half
1   (20 ounce) bag frozen cut broccoli

COMBINE all ingredients in crockpot. COVER.
COOK on LOW for 6 hours or HIGH for 3 hours.

Barbecue

To roast meat slowly on a grill or in a oven, basting frequently with a highly seasoned sauce; Not to be confused with having too much to drink.

"I have everything, but I'm still not satisfied."

TONGUE

Be self-controlled and alert. Your enemy the devil prowls around like a roaring lion looking for someone to devour.
1 Peter 5:8 (NIV)

BLONDE A.D.D. INTERPRETATION:

SATAN IS ALWAYS WANTING OUR TONGUE DON'T LET HIM HAVE YOUR LUNG

YOUR INTERPRETATION:

_____ _____ _____ _____ _____

_____ _____ _____ _____ _____

"I have everything, but I'm still not satisfied."

Beef & Cheese Soup
"Beauty & The Beef"

1½	pounds lean ground beef
½	cup onions, chopped
2	cups water
2	cups potatoes, peeled, cubed
1	(14 ounce) can whole kernel corn
1	pound process cheese spread, cubed

BROWN 1st 2 ingredients in a skillet. DRAIN.
PLACE in crockpot. ADD next 2 ingredients. COVER.
COOK on LOW for 8 hours or HIGH for 4 hours.
ADD last 2 ingredients. STIR. COOK until cheese melts.

Spicy Beef & Vegetable Soup
"Spicy & Stewed"

1½	pounds lean ground beef
1	onion, chopped
1	(10 ounce) bag frozen whole kernel corn
1	(9 ounce) bag frozen cut green beans
4	cups spicy vegetable juice
1	(14 ounce) can Italian-style stewed tomatoes
2	Tablespoons Worcestershire
1	teaspoon dried basil

BROWN 1st 2 ingredients in a skillet. DRAIN.
COMBINE all ingredients in crockpot. MIX well. COVER.
COOK on LOW for 8 hours or HIGH for 4 hours.

"I have everything, but I'm still not satisfied."

DECEIVE

The god of this age has blinded the minds of unbelievers, so that they cannot see the light of the gospel of the glory of Christ, who is the image of God.
2 Corinthians 4:4 (NIV)

BLONDE A.D.D. INTERPRETATION:

SATAN'S MISSION IS TO DECEIVE SEEK GOD YOU WILL RECEIVE

YOUR INTERPRETATION:

_____ _____ ____ _____ ____

_____ _____ ____ _____ ____

"I have everything, but I'm still not satisfied."

Chili
"No More Chili Mournings"

2	pounds lean ground beef
1	onion, chopped
	salt & pepper, to taste
3	teaspoons chili powder
2	teaspoons ground cumin
2	(15 ounce) cans diced tomatoes
2	(15 ounce) cans kidney beans, drained

BROWN 1st 2 ingredients in a skillet. DRAIN.
ADD next 4 seasonings to beef. COOK for 3 minutes.
COMBINE all ingredients in crockpot. COVER.
COOK on LOW for 6 hours or HIGH for 3 hours.

Hamburger Soup
"Grounded By The Light"

2	pounds lean ground beef
1	onion, chopped
1	(28 ounce) can crushed tomatoes
3	cans beef consomme
2	cans water
4	carrots, sliced
3	celery stalks, chopped
½	cup dried parsley
½	teaspoon thyme
	salt & pepper, to taste

BROWN 1st 2 ingredients in a large skillet. DRAIN.
COMBINE all ingredients in crockpot. COVER.
COOK on LOW for 6 hours or HIGH for 3 hours.

www.anotherblondemoment.com

"I have everything, but I'm still not satisfied."

PLANT

and provide for those who grieve in Zion— to bestow on them a crown of beauty instead of ashes, the oil of gladness instead of mourning, and a garment of praise instead of a spirit of despair. They will be called oaks of display of righteousness, a planting of the LORD for the display of his splendor.
Isaiah 61:3 (NIV)

BLONDE A.D.D. INTERPRETATION:

THE ASHES OF ALL MY PAIN
HE PLANTS RIGHTEOUSNESS FOR MY GAIN

YOUR INTERPRETATION:

____ ____ ____ ____ ____

____ ____ ____ ____ ____

Mexican Beef Soup
"Mexi He Can Mercy"

1½	pounds lean ground beef
½	cup onions, chopped
1	(10 ounce) bag frozen whole kernel corn
1	(15 ounce) can Mexican-style chili beans
1	(14 ounce) can diced stewed tomatoes
1	(10 ounce) can Minestrone soup
2	cups water

BROWN 1st 2 ingredients in a large skillet. DRAIN.
COMBINE all ingredients in crockpot. COVER.
COOK on LOW for 6 hours or HIGH for 3 hours.

Minestrone Beef Soup
"Lean Words Of Mercy"

1½	pounds lean ground beef
½	cup onions, chopped
1	(10 ounce) can diced tomatoes & green chilies
2	(10 ounce) cans Minestrone soup
2	cups water

BROWN 1st 2 ingredients in a large skillet. DRAIN.
COMBINE all ingredients in crockpot. COVER.
COOK on LOW for 6 hours or HIGH for 3 hours.

"I have everything, but I'm still not satisfied."

MERCY

Two blind men were sitting by the roadside, and when they heard that Jesus was going by, they shouted, "Lord, Son of David, have mercy on us!" Matthew 20:30 (NIV)

BLONDE A.D.D. INTERPRETATION:

I WAS BLIND IN HIS WORD BUT I ASKED AND HE HEARD

YOUR INTERPRETATION:

____ ____ ____ ____ ____

____ ____ ____ ____ ____

"I have everything, but I'm still not satisfied."

Chicken Enchilada Soup
"Chicken Little In The Flesh"

1	Rotisserie chicken, shredded
1	(1.5 ounce) Enchilada sauce mix
1	(15 ounce) can whole kernel corn
1	(10 ounce) can diced tomatoes & green chilies
2	(15 ounce) cans Ranch-style beans with jalapenos
2	(14 ounce) cans chicken broth
1	can cream of chicken soup
2	cups sour cream

COMBINE all ingredients in crockpot. COVER.
COOK on LOW for 6 hours or HIGH for 3 hours.

Italian Chicken Stew
"Stewed Chick"

4	boneless, skinless chicken breasts, cooked, cubed
3	cups water
3	chicken bouillon cubes
1	onion, chopped
3	potatoes, peeled, cubed
1	(15 ounce) can crushed seasoned tomatoes
½	teaspoon paprika
1	Tablespoon Italian seasoning
	salt & pepper, to taste
1	(8 ounce) box pasta, cooked

COMBINE 1st 10 ingredients in crockpot. MIX well.
COVER. COOK on LOW for 6 hours or HIGH for 3 hours.
ADD pasta. COOK on HIGH for 30 minutes.

"I have everything, but I'm still not satisfied."

DESIRE

Do not consider his appearance or his height, for I have rejected him. The LORD does not look at the things man looks at. Man looks at the outward appearance, but the LORD looks at the heart.
1 Samuel 16:7 (NIV)

BLONDE A.D.D. INTERPRETATION:

IT'S NOT WHAT OTHERS THINK OR WHAT YOU ACQUIRE
IT IS THE HEART: EMOTIONS, INTELLECT OF YOUR DESIRE

YOUR INTERPRETATION:

___ ___ ___ ___ ___ ___ ___ ___ ___ ___

___ ___ ___ ___ ___ ___ ___ ___ ___ ___

Mexican Chicken Soup
"Mexi He Can Renew"

3	boneless, skinless chicken breasts, cooked, cubed
4	potatoes, peeled, chopped
1	(15 ounce) jar salsa
1	(4 ounce) can diced green chilies
1	envelope dry taco seasoning mix
1	(8 ounce) can tomato sauce

COMBINE 1st 5 ingredients in crockpot.
POUR tomato sauce over ingredients. **DO NOT STIR.**
COVER. COOK on **LOW** for 6 hours or **HIGH** for 3 hours.

Chicken Noodle Soup
"Noodled Away Without HIM"

3	boneless, skinless chicken breasts, cooked, cubed
1	Tablespoon olive oil
2	celery stalks, chopped
1	onion, chopped
1	(14 ounce) can diced tomatoes
1	(14 ounce) can chicken broth
1	teaspoon thyme
1	(9 ounce) frozen green peas
1	cup frozen home-style egg noodles

COMBINE 1st 8 ingredients in crockpot. **COVER.**
COOK on **LOW** for 6 hours or **HIGH** for 3 hours.
STIR in noodles. **COVER.**
COOK on **HIGH** for 30 minutes.

DECAY

Therefore we do not lose heart. Though outwardly we are wasting away, yet inwardly we are being renewed day by day.
2 Corinthians 4:16 (NIV)

BLONDE A.D.D. INTERPRETATION:

EVEN THOUGH OUR BODY WILL DECAY
A BELIEVER'S SOUL WON'T GO AWAY

YOUR INTERPRETATION:

_____ _____ _____ _____ _____

_____ _____ _____ _____ _____

"I have everything, but I'm still not satisfied."

Chicken & Rice Gumbo
"Thigh & Breast Is Where I Rest"

4	boneless, skinless chicken breasts, cooked, cubed
$\frac{1}{4}$	pound smoked sausage, cooked, chopped
2	celery stalks, sliced
1	carrot, sliced
1	onion, chopped,
1	(14 ounce) can stewed tomatoes
5	cups water
4	chicken bouillon cubes
1	teaspoon thyme
1	(10 ounce) bag frozen cut okra
3	cups rice, cooked

COMBINE 1st 10 ingredients in crockpot. COVER.
COOK on LOW for 8 hours or HIGH for 4 hours.
SERVE over rice.

Baste

To moisten food during cooking with drippings, water or seasoned sauce, to prevent from drying, to add flavor; Not to be confused with sewing a hem.

"I have everything, but I'm still not satisfied."

DISTRACTION

But I am afraid that just as Eve was deceived by the serpent's cunning, your minds may somehow be led astray from your sincere and pure devotion to Christ.
2 Corinthians 11:3 (NIV)

BLONDE A.D.D. INTERPRETATION:

SATAN WAS REAL FOR EVE
KNOW IN CHRIST TO BELIEVE

YOUR INTERPRETATION:

_____ _____ _____ _____ _____

_____ _____ _____ _____ _____

"I have everything, but I'm still not satisfied."

Chicken & Vegetable Chowder
"Don't Be Chicken...Restore"

4	boneless, skinless chicken breasts, cooked, cubed
1	(10 ounce) bag frozen broccoli cuts
1	carrot, sliced
1	onion, chopped
1	(14 ounce) can whole kernel corn
1	(4 ounce) jar sliced mushrooms, drained
1	Tablespoon minced garlic
$\frac{1}{2}$	teaspoon thyme
1	(14 ounce) can chicken broth
1	can cream of potato soup
⅓	cup half and half

COMBINE 1st 10 ingredients in crockpot. COVER.
COOK on LOW for 6 hours or HIGH for 3 hours.
STIR in half and half. COVER.COOK on HIGH for 15 minutes.

Chicken & Wild Rice Soup
"Be Wild Not Chicken For HIS Word"

3	boneless, skinless chicken breasts, cooked, cubed
1	can cream of chicken soup
6	cups chicken broth
1	cup shredded carrots
1	(6 ounce) box long-grain & wild rice mix with seasoning
2	cups water

COMBINE all ingredients in crockpot. COVER.
COOK on HIGH for 6 hours.

"I have everything, but I'm still not satisfied."

RESTORATION

But I will restore you to health and heal your wounds, declares the LORD, because you are called an outcast, Zion for whom no one cares. Jeremiah 30:17 (NIV)

BLONDE A.D.D. INTERPRETATION:

HE RESTORES EVEN WHEN WE BACKSLIDE
HE IS THERE AT OUR SIDE

YOUR INTERPRETATION:

___ ___ ___ ___ ___

___ ___ ___ ___ ___

"I have everything, but I'm still not satisfied."

Vegetarian Chili
"Veg Out & Chill"

2	Tablespoons olive oil
1	onion, chopped
1	garlic clove, crushed
1	red bell pepper, cut in 1 inch pieces
1	green bell pepper, cut in 1 inch pieces
2	Tablespoons cumin
1	teaspoon cayenne pepper
3	(14 ounce) cans crushed tomatoes
1	(10 ounce) bag frozen whole kernel corn
4	(10 ounce) cans black beans, rinsed, drained
2	cups picante sauce

SAUTE 1st 7 ingredients in a skillet for 5 minutes.
COMBINE all ingredients in crockpot. MIX well. COVER.
COOK on LOW for 6 hours or HIGH for 3 hours.

Corn & Tomato Chowder
"Your Corny Living In Your Skin"

1	(10 ounce) bag frozen whole kernel corn
4	potatoes, peeled, cubed
2	(15 ounce) cans diced tomatoes
1½	cups water
	salt & pepper, to taste

COMBINE all ingredients in crockpot. COVER.
COOK on LOW for 6 hours or HIGH for 3 hours.

"I have everything, but I'm still not satisfied."

HEAL

Do not be wise in your own eyes; fear the LORD and shun evil. This will bring health to your body and nourishment to your bones.
Proverbs 3:7-8 (NIV)

BLONDE A.D.D. INTERPRETATION:

DON'T DO WHAT EVER YOU FEEL HIS WORD WILL SEAL THE DEAL

YOUR INTERPRETATION:

_____ _____ _____ _____ _____ _____

_____ _____ _____ _____ _____ _____

"I have everything, but I'm still not satisfied."

Corn & Potato Chowder
"Corny About Yourself"

6	turkey bacon slices
½	cup onions, chopped
2	cups potatoes, peeled, cubed
2	(10 ounce) bag frozen whole kernel corn
1	(16 ounce) can cream-style corn
1	Tablespoon Worcestershire
2	cups water
1	Tablespoon sugar
1	Tablespoon seasoned salt
1	(14 ounce) can chicken broth
1	cup milk
¼	cup margarine

FRY bacon. **CRUMBLE. REMOVE. SET ASIDE.**
SAUTE onion in bacon drippings for 5 minutes.
COMBINE 1st 10 ingredients in crockpot. **COVER.**
COOK on **LOW** for 6 hours or **HIGH** for 3 hours.
ADD last 2 ingredients. **STIR. COVER.**
COOK on **HIGH** for 30 minutes.

Beat

To work a mixture smooth with a hard movement; Not to be confused with the Michael Jackson song.

"I have everything, but I'm still not satisfied."

SELF

It is not good to eat too much honey nor is it honorable to seek one's own honor.
Proverbs 25:27 (NIV)

BLONDE A.D.D. INTERPRETATION:

TELLING EVERYONE HOW GREAT YOU ARE DOESN'T MAKE YOU THE SHINING STAR

YOUR INTERPRETATION:

____ ____ ____ ____ ____

____ ____ ____ ____ ____

"I have everything, but I'm still not satisfied."

Mushroom Cheddar Soup
"I Mushroomed Into A Believer"

½   cup margarine
1   (8 ounce) fresh sliced mushrooms
1   onion, chopped
2   celery stalks, chopped
¾   cup flour
3   (14 ounce) cans chicken broth
1½   cups heavy cream
3   cups shredded cheddar cheese
       salt & pepper, to taste
       hot sauce, to taste

SAUTE 1st 4 ingredients in large skillet for 15 minutes.
ADD flour. STIR & COAT evenly for 10 minutes.
COMBINE all ingredients in crockpot. COVER.
COOK on LOW for 4 hours or HIGH for 2 hours.

Veggie Cheese Soup
"A Holey Cheese"

1   (16 ounce) can cream-style corn
4   cups potatoes, peeled, cubed
2   carrots, sliced
½   cup onions, chopped
2   (14 ounce) cans chicken broth
1   pound process cheese spread, cubed

COMBINE 1st 5 ingredients in crockpot. COVER.
COOK on LOW for 10 hours or HIGH for 5 hours.
ADD cheese. COVER. COOK until cheese melts.

www.anotherblondemoment.com

"I have everything, but I'm still not satisfied."

REBORN

and to put on the new self, created to be like God in true righteousness and holiness.
Ephesians 4:24 (NIV)

BLONDE A.D.D. INTERPRETATION:

IT TOOK OBEDIENCE AND TIME FOR THE OLD SELF TO GO AWAY THE NEW SELF CAME IN READING HIS WORD AND WHEN I PRAY

YOUR INTERPRETATION:

___ ___ ___ ___ ___ ___ ___ ___ ___ ___ ___

___ ___ ___ ___ ___ ___ ___ ___ ___ ___ ___

"I have everything, but I'm still not satisfied."

Split Pea Soup
"A Split Decision"

1	(16 ounce) dried green split peas, rinsed
2	cups ham, diced
3	carrots, sliced
1	onion, chopped
2	celery stalks, chopped
2	garlic cloves, crushed
1	bay leaf
1	Tablespoon seasoned salt
$\frac{1}{2}$	teaspoon pepper
$1\frac{1}{2}$	quarts hot water

LAYER all ingredients in crockpot in order given.
DO NOT STIR. COVER.
COOK on LOW for 10 hours or HIGH for 5 hours.

Potato Chowder
"Chow Down On HIS Word"

6	potatoes, peeled, cubed
1	onion, chopped
3	(14 ounce) cans chicken broth
1	can cream of chicken soup
1	(8 ounce) cream cheese, cubed
10	turkey bacon slices, cooked, crumbled

COMBINE 1st 4 ingredients in crockpot. COVER.
COOK on LOW for 10 hours or HIGH for 5 hours.
STIR in remaining 2 ingredients.
COOK on HIGH for 20 minutes.

"I have everything, but I'm still not satisfied."

MONEY

"No servant can serve two masters. Either he will hate the one and love the other, or he will be devoted to the one and despise the other. You cannot serve both God and Money."
Luke 16:13 (NIV)

BLONDE A.D.D. INTERPRETATION

LOVING BOTH GOD AND MONEY YOU CAN'T DO YOUR WEALTH WILL BE GIVEN INSIDE OF YOU

YOUR INTERPRETATION:

___ __ _ __ __ __ __ __ ___ ___

___ __ _ __ __ __ __ __ ___ ___

"I have everything, but I'm still not satisfied."

Black Bean Pork Soup
"Bean Receiving Some Pork"

1	pound boneless pork, cubed
2	(16 ounce) cans black beans, drained
1	bell pepper, chopped
1	tomato, chopped
1	red onion, thinly sliced
1	garlic clove, crushed
½	teaspoon ground cumin
2	teaspoons chili powder
½	teaspoon salt
1	(6 ounce) can tomato sauce
½	cup sour cream
2	Tablespoons cilantro, chopped

COMBINE all ingredients in crockpot. COVER.
COOK on LOW for 8 hours or HIGH for 4 hours.

White Bean Ham Soup
"Bean Receiving More Ham"

1	pound dry white beans, washed
8	cups water
2	cups ham, diced
1	onion, chopped
3	celery stalks, chopped
2	Tablespoons dried parsley
	salt & pepper, to taste

COMBINE all ingredients in crockpot. COVER.
COOK on LOW for 10 hours or HIGH for 5 hours.

www.anotherblondemoment.com

"I have everything, but I'm still not satisfied."

CHOKE

but the worries of this life, the deceitfulness of wealth and the desires for other things come in and choke the word, making it unfruitful.
Mark 4:19 (NIV)

BLONDE A.D.D. INTERPRETATION

DON'T BE SHALLOW AND LET MATERIAL THINGS CHOKE OUT THE WORD OF THE KING

YOUR INTERPRETATION:

_____ _____ ____ _____ ____ ____ ____ ____

_____ ____ ____ _____ ____ ____ ____ _____

"I have everything, but I'm still not satisfied."

Italian Sausage Soup
"Submit Chopped"

1	pound Italian sausage, sliced
1	onion, chopped
1	bell pepper, cut in ½ inch slices
1	(14 ounce) can diced tomatoes with juice
1	(15 ounce) Northern beans
2	(14 ounce) cans beef broth

BROWN 1st 3 ingredients in skillet. DRAIN.
COMBINE all ingredients in crockpot. COVER.
COOK on LOW for 4 hours or HIGH for 2 hours.

Smoked Sausage Chowder
"Smoked Out Satan"

1	pound Polish Kielbasa, sliced
1	cup mild green chilie picante sauce
1	garlic clove, crushed
1	(10 ounce) bag frozen whole kernel corn
1	tomato, chopped
2	(14 ounce) cans chicken broth
1	(15 ounce) can garbanzo beans, drained
2	Tablespoons fresh cilantro, chopped
¼	teaspoon crushed dried red pepper

COMBINE all ingredients in crockpot. MIX well. COVER.
COOK on LOW for 6 hours or HIGH for 3 hours.

"I have everything, but I'm still not satisfied."

SUBMIT

Submit yourselves, then, to God. Resist the devil, and he will flee from you.
James 4:7 (NIV)

BLONDE A.D.D. INTERPRETATION:

STAY IN LINE WITH GOD'S CALLING WITH SATAN YOU WILL BE FALLING

YOUR INTERPRETATION:

_____ _____ _____ _____ _____ _____

_____ _____ _____ _____ _____ _____

"I have everything, but I'm still not satisfied."

Seafood Chowder
"ReNew Your Food, SEE!"

1	can cream of potato soup
1	can cream of mushroom soup
2½	cups milk
4	carrots, sliced
2	potatoes, peeled, cubed
1	onion, chopped
2	celery stalks, chopped
1	teaspoon salt
1	teaspoon pepper
2	(6 ounce) cans shrimp, drained
1	(6 ounce) can crab meat
6	turkey bacon strips, cooked, crumbled

COMBINE 1st 9 ingredients in crockpot. COVER.
COOK on LOW for 4 hours or HIGH for 2 hours.
ADD last 4 ingredients. COVER.
COOK on HIGH for 30 minutes.

Blend

To mix two or more ingredients until smooth;
Not to be confused with a blended family.

"I have everything, but I'm still not satisfied."

WEALTH

Whoever loves money never has money enough; whoever loves wealth is never satisfied with his income. This too is meaningless.
Ecclesiastes 5:10 (NIV)

BLONDE A.D.D. INTERPRETATION:

I USE TO THINK MONEY MADE ME HAPPY
BUT REAL TRUE HAPPINESS COMES FROM MY PAPPY

YOUR INTERPRETATION:

___ ___ ___ ___ ___ ___ ___

___ ___ ___ ___ ___ ___ ___ ___

"I have everything, but I'm still not satisfied."

Spicy Shrimp Chowder
"Chow Down For The Lord"

1	onion, chopped
1	teaspoon margarine
1	(12 ounce) can evaporated milk
1	can cream of potato soup
2	cans cream of chicken soup
1	can white corn, drained
1	teaspoon Creole seasoning
$\frac{1}{4}$	teaspoon garlic powder
1	pound shrimp, cooked, peeled
1	(3 ounce) package cream cheese, cubed

SAUTE' 1st 2 ingredients in a skillet.
COMBINE onion & next 6 ingredients in crockpot.
COVER. COOK on LOW for 3 hours or HIGH for 1½ hours.
STIR in last 2 ingredients. COOK on HIGH for 30 minutes.

Cream

To rub, whip or beat with a spoon until mixture is soft and fluffy; Not to be confused with what you put in your coffee.

PROVIDING AND EMPOWERING

Keep your lives free from the love of money and be content with what you have, because God has said, "Never will I leave you; never will I forsake you."
Hebrews 13:5 (NIV)

I used to want everything I saw
Clothes, Jewelry, Cars were my flaw.

I always wondered how others had more than me
I would always give my husband the third degree.

As I began learning what life was really all about
It wasn't about buying, doing or having clout.

I was like Miriam jealous of what others had
When I finally realized this, I was sad.

I was like Uzziah the King full of pride
Through my pain, I finally asked HIM to guide.

HIS cleansing and me working on turning away from sin
Is allowing me to turn from sin to win.

GOD provides ways for me to have a mature belief
Christ's Spirit is empowering me, what a relief.

SIDES

When we acknowledge HIM, our fruit will be abundant.

FRUIT OF THE SPIRIT

"I have everything, but I'm still not satisfied."

Yes, I know this a cookbook about a Crockpot. And yes, I am blonde like Debbie. But I am going to turn the temperature down on the Crockpot for a moment and talk about trees and fruit.

Have you ever gone out and picked apples from an apple tree? There really is no prettier fruit than a shiny red apple. But that fruit didn't come from just any ole tree. It came from a tree planted in good soil and watered frequently. Let's just say an apple represents love. My basket was full of beautiful fruit. The most beautiful fruit in my basket was the love my Mom gave to me and my family. This love was a product of the love she had for our Heavenly Father.

Because of that love, our basket overflowed with joy, peace, patience, kindness, goodness, faithfulness, gentleness and self-control. My Mom shared her fruit with me throughout my entire life. She also shared her fruit with many others.

When I was 24 my Mom was diagnosed with stage 4 cancer. This was the most devastating news I had ever received. But, on her journey with this illness God blessed her with the opportunity to share her fruit with many.

Throughout her journey God revealed so much about himself to me. Watching my Mom embark on this journey was a very difficult thing to do. As she stepped down this path He set before her, He filled her basket full of all of His fruit. He allowed her the opportunity to share her fruit with all of those she knew and loved. You see, God had planted her firmly in His soil, so she could bear His fruit.

Like I said in the beginning, in order to produce great fruit, we must be planted firmly in good soil. Psalms 1:3 says- **"He is like a tree planted in good soil by streams of water, which yields its fruit in season and whose leaf does not wither. Whatever he does prospers."**

My heart's desire is to be the tree described by the Psalmist. My Mom was a beautiful tree planted in the garden of my life and I am so blessed to be one of her branches.

Now, before you go turn the heat back up on that Crockpot......

Are you planted firmly in His soil? What's in your basket? My prayer is that your basket is full of His beautiful fruit.

"You shall know them by their fruits." Matthew 7:16

Anne Marie Tipton

When we acknowledge HIM, our fruit will be abundant.

SIDES

When we acknowledge HIM, our fruit will be abundant.

FRUIT OF THE SPIRIT

Asparagus Crockpoted
"He Spared Us Our Sins"

2	cans cut up asparagus, drained
1	can cream of asparagus soup
1	cup shredded cheddar cheese
1	egg, hard-boiled, thinly sliced
½	cup saltine crackers, crushed
2	teaspoons margarine

PLACE asparagus in cooking sprayed crockpot.
COMBINE next 2 ingredients in a bowl.
TOP asparagus with egg, soup mixture, cracker crumbs.
DOT with margarine. COVER.
COOK on LOW for 4 hours or HIGH for 2 hours.

Black Beans Crockpoted
"I've Bean Loved And Set Free"

5	turkey bacon slices, cooked, crumbled
2	(16 ounce) cans black beans, drained
½	bell pepper, chopped
½	onion, chopped
1½	teaspoons mustard
½	cup ketchup
½	cup barbecue sauce
½	cup brown sugar

COMBINE all ingredients in crockpot. MIX well.
COVER. COOK on LOW for 4 hours or HIGH for 2 hours.

When we acknowledge HIM, our fruit will be abundant.

LOVE

This is love: not that we loved God, but that he loved us and sent his Son as an atoning sacrifice for our sins.
1 John 4:8 (NIV)

BLONDE A.D.D. INTERPRETATION:

I LIVED 48 YEARS ALL ABOUT ME REAL LOVE FROM JESUS SET ME FREE

YOUR INTERPRETATION:

___ __ __ __ ___ ___ ___ ___ __

___ __ __ __ ___ ___ ___ ___ __

When we acknowledge HIM, our fruit will be abundant.

Green Beans & Tomatoes
"I've Bean Patient & Kind"

1	(16 ounce) can cut string beans
1	garlic clove, crushed
1	(15 ounce) can diced tomatoes
½	cup onion, chopped
½	teaspoon oregano
1	teaspoon lemon juice
1	Tablespoon olive oil
½	teaspoon pepper

COMBINE all ingredients in crockpot. MIX well.
COVER.COOK on LOW for 4 hours or HIGH for 2 hours.

Cheesy Green Beans
"It's Cheesy Beaning Jealous"

3	(14 ounce) cans green beans, drained
½	cup onion, chopped
2	Tablespoons margarine
2	Tablespoons flour
1	teaspoon salt
2	cups shredded Monterey Jack cheese

COMBINE 1st 5 ingredients in crockpot. MIX well.
COVER.COOK on LOW for 4 hours or HIGH for 2 hours.
ADD cheese. COOK on HIGH for 30 minutes.

When we acknowledge HIM, our fruit will be abundant.

LOVE

When I read the verse 'love God with all your heart, soul and mind'
I wondered why I didn't love this imaginary being, why was I blind?

I knew HE was something different because that is what I was told
I knew if I was going to change my life, I had to take hold.

I remember hearing other people say how much they loved the Lord
I wondered why those words were so easy to be ignored.

I went to church, I said my prayers, I read many devotions
I raised my children, I worked hard, I went through the motions.

When I was 47 I felt something different inside I can't explain
On a cold, sunny, February day I remember dropping my chains.

I called my daughter and told her I felt like the Incredible Hulk
I was tired of blaming other people and sitting around to sulk.

As I began understanding what I was reading in HIS word
My life had a different meaning something inside of me was spurred.

I remember getting it, understanding what HE was saying
My actions were responding to what I read, I was always praying.

It is like being with a friend who is really, really smart
I was developing a relationship with someone in my heart.

Sanctification was a word I never understood, could I be a receiver
I was being made HOLY and my lifestyle was changing into a believer.

When we acknowledge HIM, our fruit will be abundant.

Horseradish Green Beans
"Don't Horse Around With Joy"

3   (14 ounce) cans green beans, drained
4   teaspoons prepared mustard
2   teaspoons prepared horseradish
2   Tablespoons brown sugar

COMBINE all ingredients in crockpot. COVER.
COOK on LOW for 4 hours or HIGH for 2 hours.

Cheesy Broccoli & Cauliflower
"A Call For Flowery Joy"

1   (10 ounce) bag frozen cauliflower
1   (10 ounce) bag frozen broccoli
4   turkey bacon slices, cooked, crumbled
1   can cheddar cheese soup
      salt & pepper, to taste
1   cup shredded cheddar cheese

COMBINE 1st 6 ingredients in crockpot in order given.
COVER.COOK on LOW for 6 hours or HIGH for 3 hours.
ADD cheese. COOK on HIGH for 20 minutes.

When we acknowledge HIM, our fruit will be abundant.

JOY

Let us fix our eyes on Jesus, the author and perfecter of our faith, who for the joy set before him endured the cross, scorning its shame, and sat down at the right hand of the throne of God.
Hebrews 12:2 (NIV)

BLONDE A.D.D. INTERPRETATION:

CHRIST SHED HIS BLOOD FOR MY SHAME
STAYING IN HIS WORD HELPS ME PROCLAIM

YOUR INTERPRETATION:

___ ___ ___ ___ ___ ___ ___ ___

___ ___ ___ ___ ___ ___ ___ ___

When we acknowledge HIM, our fruit will be abundant.

Broccoli & Rice Crockpoted
"Joy Riced Down in My Heart"

1	onion, chopped
$\frac{1}{4}$	cup margarine
2	cups Minute Rice
2	cups water
1	can cream of mushroom soup
$\frac{1}{2}$	teaspoon salt
1	(18 ounce) jar Cheez Whiz
1	(16 ounce) bag frozen chopped broccoli

COMBINE all ingredients in crockpot. MIX well.
COVER. COOK on LOW for 6 hours or HIGH for 3 hours.

Broccoli Souffle
"Souffle For Joy"

1	(16 ounce) bag frozen chopped broccoli
1	can cream of celery soup
1	cup mayonnaise
3	Tablespoons onion, finely chopped
2	eggs, beaten
1	cup shredded cheddar cheese
15	buttery crackers, crushed
1	stick margarine

COOK broccoli according to directions. DRAIN.
COMBINE 1st 6 ingredients in cooking sprayed crockpot.
COMBINE last 2 ingredients. SPRINKLE over mixture.
COOK on LOW for 4 hours or HIGH for 2 hours.

When we acknowledge HIM, our fruit will be abundant.

JOY

Pain is when I see my children hurt.
My prayers to God is for them to convert.

Change their heart of their pride, greed and actions
Allowing satan not to have any satisfaction.

If I'm not in God's word I don't know how to parent
My skills come from how I was raised, that's apparent.

I kept doing what I was taught and passing it down
Not willing to accept His recipe, I went round and round.

Round and round, giving my own thoughts
Knowing the story of Christ, but was it really bought.

Was it just a story told long ago, not affecting me
That is exactly what satan wanted me to see.

Accept the story and choose to live a different life
Or I could choose to live a life full of strife.

For forty seven years I chose strife over joy
Now my obedience to Him enjoy

His strength, His love, His humor and what is beyond
Showing His love through a cookbook is really BLONDE.

I have asked for forgiveness of my parenting skills
Guiltless and free is now what I feel.

When we acknowledge HIM, our fruit will be abundant.

Corn Pudding
"Pudding Peace In HIM"

$\frac{1}{4}$	cup sugar
$\frac{1}{4}$	cup flour
1	teaspoon salt
4	eggs, beaten
2	cups milk
4	cups frozen whole kernel corn

COMBINE 1st 3 ingredients in cooking sprayed crockpot.
COMBINE next 2 ingredients. STIR in floured mixture.
ADD corn. COVER. COOK on HIGH for 6 hours.

Jalapeno Mexican Corn
"Corny For HIM"

2	eggs, beaten
1	cup sour cream
$\frac{1}{4}$	cup margarine, melted
$\frac{1}{2}$	onion, chopped
1	(11 ounce) can Mexi-corn, drained
1	(14 ounce) can cream-style corn
3	Tablespoons diced jalapenos
1	(8 ounce) box cornbread mix

COMBINE all ingredients in a bowl.
POUR in cooking sprayed crockpot. MIX well.
COVER.COOK on LOW for 4 hours or HIGH for 2 hours.

When we acknowledge HIM, our fruit will be abundant.

PEACE

"I have told you these things, so that in me you may have peace. In this world you will have trouble. But take heart! I have overcome the world."
John 16:33 (NIV)

BLONDE A.D.D. INTERPRETATION:

EVEN THOUGH WE HAVE PAIN AND STRUGGLES CRAWL UP WITH CHRIST AND JUST SNUGGLE

YOUR INTERPRETATION:

____ ____ ____ ____ ____ ____ ____ ____

____ ____ ____ ____ ____ ____ ____

When we acknowledge HIM, our fruit will be abundant.

Eggplant Parmesan
"Planting With Peace"

2	eggplants, peeled, cut ½-inch slices
	salt, to taste
2	eggs, beaten
¼	cup water
3	Tablespoons flour
	olive oil
1	cup seasoned bread crumbs
1	cup Parmesan cheese
1	(32 ounce) marinara sauce
1	(16 ounce) sliced Mozzarella cheese

PLACE eggplant in a bowl in layers.
SPRINKLE each layer of eggplant with salt.
COMBINE next 3 ingredients in a bowl.
DIP eggplant slices in batter.
BROWN eggplant in oil in a skillet.
COMBINE bread crumbs & cheese in a bowl.
LAYER ¼ eggplant, ¼ crumb mixture, ¼ Mozzarella.
REPEAT to makes 4 layers of eggplant.
COVER. COOK on **LOW** for 8 hours or **HIGH** for 4 hours.

Cut in

To mix shortening with dry ingredients using a knife or fork; Not to be confused with pulling out in front of someone in a car, or what is done when painting.

When we acknowledge HIM, our fruit will be abundant.

PEACE

If only I looked better on the outside
Peace would have come on the inside.

If only I had a ring and necklace with a great big diamond
Peace would have come and I wouldn't have felt shunned.

If only I hadn't used those words that hurt
Peace would have come, I wouldn't have felt like dirt.

If only I hadn't used wine to numb my pain
Peace would have come and given me no shame.

If only I had a nice home, fancy car and expensive clothes
Peace would have come and I wouldn't have these holes.

Peace didn't come to me in things or feelings
Peace came to me in the transformation of my healing.

Peace is talking to God when you don't need a thing
Our time is all He is asking us to bring.

Peace is reading His word and when I finally understand
His character, His love, His fruit, begin to expand.

Peace is like a river taking His course into the sea
Peace is what God is bringing over me.

When we
acknowledge HIM,
our fruit will be
abundant.

Brown Sugar Fruit
"Fruity For Patience"

1	(29 ounce) can pear halves, drained
1	(29 ounce) can peach halves, drained
2	(16 ounce) cans apricot halves, drained
1	(20 ounce) can pineapple chunks, drained
1	(3 ounce) package sliced almonds
1	(20 ounce) can pineapple slices, drained
1½	cups brown sugar
½	cup margarine, melted

LAYER 1st 6 ingredients in crockpot in order given.
COMBINE last 2 ingredients in a bowl. POUR over fruit.
COVER. COOK on LOW for 6 hours or HIGH for 3 hours.

Macaroni & Cheese
"Elbowed With Patience"

2	cups elbow macaroni, cooked, drained
4	cups shredded sharp cheddar cheese
1	(13 ounce) can evaporated milk
1½	cups milk
2	eggs, beaten
1	teaspoon salt
½	teaspoon black pepper

COMBINE all ingredients in cooking sprayed crockpot.
MIX well. COVER.
COOK on LOW for 4 hours or HIGH for 2 hours.
(DO NOT REMOVE TOP OR STIR UNTIL IT HAS
FINISHED)

PATIENCE

because you know that the testing of your faith develops perseverance.
James 1:3 (NIV)

BLONDE A.D.D. INTERPRETATION:

WHEN TIMES GET TOUGH YOUR NOT ALONE
PATIENCE, DON'T DO IT OWN YOUR OWN

YOUR INTERPRETATION:

___ ___ ___ ___ ___ ___ ___ ___

___ ___ ___ ___ ___ ___ ___ ___

Cheesy Hash Brown Potatoes
" Waiting Isn't Cheesy"

1   can cream of mushroom soup
1   cup sour cream
2   cups shredded Colby Jack cheese
1   (32 ounce) frozen hash brown potatoes, thawed

COMBINE all ingredients in cooking sprayed crockpot.
COVER. COOK on LOW for 8 hours or HIGH for 4 hours.

Cream Cheese Potatoes
"Creaming For Patience"

1   (32 ounce) frozen hash brown potatoes, thawed
2   Tablespoons margarine
1   onion, chopped
1   cup sour cream
1   Tablespoon flour
1   (8 ounce) cream cheese, cubed
$\frac{1}{2}$ cup grated Parmesan cheese
$\frac{1}{2}$ cup evaporated milk
1   can cream of potato soup
$\frac{1}{4}$ teaspoon pepper
$\frac{1}{2}$ teaspoon dried thyme leaves

PLACE all ingredients in cooking sprayed crockpot.
COVER.COOK on LOW for 8 hours or HIGH for 4 hours.
STIR 1 time while cooking.

When we acknowledge HIM, our fruit will be abundant.

PATIENCE

Stressful, Angry and Frustrated is how I chose to live
Until I asked Jesus to come on in and forgive.

I didn't like how I felt not in control
Telling them how they were wrong, was my goal.

I didn't understand why they didn't think like me
I was right, they were wrong, why couldn't they just see.

Why couldn't I convince them to change their mind
Was it the way they were raised, why were they so blind.

If I had to beg, borrow and steal, not literally
Begging for them to understand my point you see.

Maybe borrowing from someone they admired
Getting them to know I was right, is what I desired.

My words were stealing their heart and caused them pain
I would use hurtful words, for my gain.

As I listen for His voice to teach me some patience
I am learning in His word and I don't feel so dense.

Ranch Hash Brown Potatoes
"Hashed Out My Kindness"

1	(32 ounce) frozen hash brown potatoes, thawed
2	(8 ounce) cream cheese, cubed
2	envelopes dry Ranch dressing mix
2	cans cream of potato soup
1	teaspoon salt
1	teaspoon pepper

COMBINE all ingredients in crockpot. MIX well.
COVER.COOK on LOW for 8 hours or HIGH or 4 hours.

Baked Potatoes Crockpoted
"Waiting To Be Kind"

10	whole russet potatoes, washed, not peeled
2	Tablespoons olive oil

RUB each potato with oil. WRAP potatoes in foil.
PLACE potatoes in crockpot. COVER.
COOK on LOW for 8 hours or HIGH for 4 hours.

Boil

To cook in boiling liquid in which bubbles rise vigorously to the surface; Not to be confused with an agitated emotional state.

When we acknowledge HIM, our fruit will be abundant.

KINDNESS

But love your enemies, do good to them, and lend to them without expecting to get anything back. Then your reward will be great, and you will be sons of the Most High, because he is kind to the ungrateful and wicked.
Luke 6:35 (NIV)

BLONDE A.D.D. INTERPRETATION:

IF SOMEONE IS MEAN TO YOU TRY TO BE SWEET AND TRUE

YOUR INTERPRETATION:

_____ _____ _____ _____ _____ _____

_____ _____ _____ _____ _____

When we acknowledge HIM, our fruit will be abundant.

Italian New Potatoes
"New Italian Relationship"

24	small new red potatoes, unpeeled
4	Tablespoons olive oil
2	envelopes zesty Italian dressing mix

POUR oil in a plastic bag. **ADD** potatoes. **COAT**.
ADD dressing mix. **SHAKE** until coated.
POUR potatoes in crockpot. **COVER**.
COOK on **LOW** for 8 hours or **HIGH** for 4 hours.

Ranch Red Potatoes
"Ranching For Kindness"

1	pound small red potatoes, unpeeled, quartered
1	(8 ounce) cream cheese, softened
1	envelope dry buttermilk ranch dressing mix
1	can condensed cream of potato soup

PLACE potatoes in crockpot.
COMBINE last 3 ingredients in a bowl. **MIX** well.
SPOON over potatoes. **COVER**.
COOK on **LOW** for 8 hours or **HIGH** for 4 hours.

Brown
To cook food quickly on top of the stove; Not to be confused with the color you get when you lay out in the sun.

KINDNESS

Helping someone when I'm not in the mood
Being genuinely kind and not being rude.

Going out of my way for someone I don't know
That is the love of GOD that I can show.

Sitting with someone when they have pain
Not wanting anything or having anything to gain.

Being able to love and I don't know why
Feeling a love that I can't deny.

Baking a cake for someone or maybe even dinner
In my heart I know I am a winner.

Asking someone if there is anything I can do
So their life that moment won't be blue.

Love is kind I can feel it in my heart
GOD is love and now I am a part.

When we acknowledge HIM, our fruit will be abundant.

Potato Salad
"Sliced With Goodness"

4	potatoes, peeled, quartered
3	celery stalks, chopped
1	bell pepper, chopped
$\frac{1}{4}$	cup balsamic vinegar
$\frac{1}{4}$	cup olive oil
	salt & pepper, to taste
2	teaspoons dried parsley
6	turkey bacon slices, cooked, crumbled

COMBINE 1st 7 ingredients in crockpot. MIX well.
COVER. COOK on LOW for 8 hours or HIGH for 4 hours.
ADD last 2 ingredients to potato mixture. COVER.
COOK on HIGH for 15 minutes.

Coconut Sweet Potatoes
"Truthful & Sweet"

2	pounds sweet potatoes, peeled, cubed
$\frac{1}{4}$	cup brown sugar
$\frac{1}{4}$	cup margarine, melted
$\frac{1}{4}$	cup flaked coconut
$\frac{1}{4}$	cup pecans, chopped
$\frac{1}{4}$	teaspoon cinnamon
$\frac{1}{4}$	teaspoon coconut extract
$\frac{1}{4}$	teaspoon vanilla

COMBINE all ingredients in crockpot. MIX well.
COVER. COOK on LOW for 8 hours or HIGH for 4 hours.

When we acknowledge HIM, our fruit will be abundant.

GOODNESS

Make a tree good and its fruit will be good, or make a tree bad and its fruit will be bad, for a tree is recognized by its fruit.
Matthew 12:33 (NIV)

BLONDE A.D.D. INTERPRETATION:

AN APPLE WITH A WORM
IT WILL MAKE YOU SQUIRM

YOUR INTERPRETATION:

_____ _____ _____ _____ _____

_____ _____ _____ _____ _____

When we acknowledge HIM, our fruit will be abundant.

Peachy Sweet Potatoes
"Peachy & Good"

2	pounds sweet potatoes, peeled, cubed
1	(20 ounce) can peach pie filling
2	Tablespoons margarine, melted
¼	teaspoon salt

COMBINE all ingredients in cooking sprayed crockpot.
MIX well. COVER.
COOK on LOW for 8 hours or HIGH for 4 hours.

Rice & Portabella Mushrooms
"Pilaf With Goodness"

¾	cup wild rice
½	cup long grain brown rice
4	portabella mushrooms, cut 1-inch slices
1	can cream of mushroom soup
1½	cups water
¼	teaspoon pepper
1	teaspoon salt

COMBINE all ingredients in crockpot. MIX well.
COVER. COOK on LOW for 5 hours or HIGH for 2½
hours.

When we acknowledge HIM, our fruit will be abundant.

GOODNESS

Love is goodness when I feel it and don't know why
When I look at a friend and I want to cry.

Goodness brings joy I can't explain why
It is a feeling of happiness I can't deny.

Goodness brings peace that is deep within
I don't have to work at not trying to sin.

Patience is good letting others go first
Not worrying about myself having thirst.

Goodness and Kindness I believe are kind of the same
With both of these I will have no shame.

Goodness is being faithful to HIS call
Knowing with HIM I will never fall.

Gentleness is good with a sweet touch or look
It's not getting mad because I have to cook.

Goodness is having a good ole soul
It is all about self-control.

Goodness is the best fruit on the tree
I pray GOD will give it to me.

Spinach & Cheese Crockpoted
"Spin & Ache For Faith"

1	loaf French bread, buttered, cubed
1	(16 ounce) bag frozen spinach
10	turkey bacon slices, cooked, crumbled
4	cups shredded cheddar cheese
	salt & pepper, to taste
1	can cream of mushroom soup
½	cup evaporated milk
5	eggs, beaten

LAYER ½ of the 1st 6 ingredients, in order given.
REPEAT layers. **COMBINE** last 3 ingredients in a bowl.
CHILL at least 1 hour. **POUR** over French bread mixture.
COVER. COOK on **LOW** for 4 hours or **HIGH** for 2 hours.

Squash Crockpoted
"Squashed With Faith"

5	squash, sliced
½	cup margarine, melted
1	can cream of chicken soup
2	slices of bread, cubed
1	cup sour cream

PLACE 1st 2 ingredients in crockpot. **COVER.**
COOK on **LOW** for 2 hours or **HIGH** for 1 hour.
ADD last 3 ingredients. **COVER. COOK** until bubbly.

When we acknowledge HIM, our fruit will be abundant.

FAITHFULNESS

So then, those who suffer according to God's will should commit themselves to their faithful Creator and continue to do good.
1 Peter 4:19 (NIV)

BLONDE A.D.D INTERPRETATION:

JESUS COMMITED HIMSELF FOR OUR SINS
HIS WORD IS WHERE IT BEGINS

YOUR INTERPRETATION:

_____ _____ _____ _____ _____ _____

_____ _____ _____ _____ _____

Corn Bread Stuffing
"Stuffed With Faith"

2	Teaspoon olive oil
1	onion, chopped
3	garlic cloves, minced
2	cups frozen whole kernel corn
1	(16 ounce) cornbread stuffing mix
$\frac{1}{4}$	cup margarine, melted
$\frac{1}{2}$	teaspoon dried thyme
1	(14 ounce) can chicken broth
1	cup shredded Colby cheese
$\frac{1}{2}$	cup grated Parmesan cheese
1	cup cashew pieces

SAUTE' 1st 3 ingredients in a skillet for 5 minutes.
COMBINE onion mixture with next 5 ingredients in crockpot.
COVER. COOK on LOW for 4 hours or HIGH for 2 hours.
STIR last 3 ingredients in with stuffing mixture. COVER.
COOK on HIGH until cheese is melted.

Walnut Stuffing
"Stuffed Nutty With Faith"

1	stick margarine
1	cup walnuts, chopped
1	onion, chopped
1	(14 ounce) cubed herbed seasoned stuffing mix
$1\frac{1}{2}$	cups applesauce
$1\frac{1}{2}$	cups water

SAUTE' 1st 3 ingredients in a skillet for 5 minutes.
COMBINE all ingredients in crockpot. MIX well.
COVER. COOK on LOW for 4 hours or HIGH for 2 hours.

FAITHFULNESS

Being Faithful is staying steadfast in what I believe
Knowing no matter what happens, HE will never leave.

Undeviating to what I know is true
Knowing everyday that HE will renew.

Not being fickle and wavering from what I know
Reading HIS word everyday so I can grow.

Being dedicated, devoted to the one I love
Conscientious of HIS word from up above.

God's faithfulness to me is HIS grace
HIS word, our heart and mind must embrace.

The strength to be faithful is HIS son
HIS strength will make living fun.

If I yield to be faithful and obedient
I will receive the greatest ingredient.

Stewed Tomatoes
"Stew Gently"

4	(14 ounce) cans tomato wedges, drained
2	Tablespoons margarine
1	onion, thinly sliced
2	celery stalks, chopped
1	bell pepper, chopped
3	Tablespoons sugar
1	bay leaf

COMBINE all ingredients in crockpot. MIX well.
COOK on LOW for 6 hours or HIGH for 3 hours.

Italian Vegetables
"Gently Veg Out"

1	teaspoon salt
1	eggplant, cut in 1-inch cubes
2	zucchini, halved, sliced ½-inch thick
1	onion, thinly sliced
1	(8 ounce) fresh sliced mushrooms
1	Tablespoon olive oil
4	tomatoes, sliced ¼-inch thick
1½	cups shredded Mozzarella cheese
2	cups tomato sauce
1	teaspoon oregano

SAUTE' 1st 7 ingredients in a large skillet until tender.
LAYER ⅓ eggplant mixture, ⅓ cheese, ⅓ tomato sauce in crockpot.
REPEAT layers. Sprinkle with oregano. COVER.
COOK on LOW for 6 hours or HIGH for 3 hours.

GENTLENESS

Take my yoke upon you and learn from me, for I am gentle and humble in heart, and you will find rest for your souls. Matthew 11:29 (NIV)

By the meekness and gentleness of Christ, I appeal to you—I, Paul, who am "timid" when face to face with you, but "bold" when away. 2 Corinthians 10:1 (NIV)

Let your gentleness be evident to all. The Lord is near. Philippians 4:5 (NIV)

Be completely humble and gentle; be patient, bearing with one another in love. Ephesians 4:2 (NIV)

Therefore, as God's chosen people, holy and dearly loved, clothe yourselves with compassion, kindness, humility, gentleness and patience. Colossians 3:12 (NIV)

As apostles of Christ we could have been a burden to you, but we were gentle among you, like a mother caring for her little children. 1 Thessalonians 2:7 (NIV)

But you, man of God, flee from all this, and pursue righteousness, godliness, faith, love, endurance and gentleness.
1 Timothy 6:11 (NIV)

And the Lord's servant must not quarrel; instead, he must be kind to everyone, able to teach, not resentful.
2 Timothy 2:24 (NIV)

Instead, it should be that of your inner self, the unfading beauty of a gentle and quiet spirit, which is of great worth in God's sight.
1 Peter 3:4 (NIV)

Mixed Vegetables
"Mixed Out Of Control"

2	(10 ounce) bags frozen mixed vegetables
2	celery stalks, chopped
2	cans cream of celery soup
½	teaspoon seasoned salt
1	envelope dry onion soup mix
½	cup water
2	Tablespoons margarine, melted

COMBINE all ingredients in crockpot. MIX well.
COVER. COOK on LOW for 4 hours or HIGH for 2 hours.

Italian Zucchini
"Controlling Our Zucchini"

8	zucchini, unpeeled, cut ¼-inch slices
1	onion, thinly sliced, separated into rings
3	Tablespoons olive oil
2	garlic cloves, crushed
2	teaspoons dried basil
2	Tablespoons dried parsley
½	cup grated Parmesan cheese
2	tomatoes, peeled, quartered

COMBINE 1st 6 ingredients in crockpot. MIX well. COVER.
COOK on LOW for 8 hours or HIGH for 4 hours.
ADD last 2 ingredients. COOK on HIGH for 15 minutes.

When we acknowledge HIM, our fruit will be abundant.

SELF-CONTROL

The fruit of love is not just a feeling or emotion
It is a decision to love GOD with a devotion.

The fruit of joy gives spiritual strength
Knowing GOD's word helps me go to any length.

The fruit of peace is believing and trusting in GOD
Refusing to live in guilt, no longer is odd.

The fruit of patience is constant in any circumstance
How I act while I am waiting is what will enhance.

The fruit of kindness is freedom from arrogance or pride
A meek and quiet spirit is what is inside.

The fruit of goodness is GOD leading me to repent
Having the knowledge and practicing what HE has sent.

The fruit of faith is required in my daily living
Through HIS word HE will keep on giving.

The fruit of gentleness is pure and at peace
As I get closer to GOD my fruit will increase.

The fruit of self-control is in my heart, mind and spirit
If I read and LISTEN I will hear it.

For 47 years I tried to bear fruit on my own
Now that my branch is on HIS vine, I am not alone.

"I know about GOD, but do I KNOW GOD?"

Faith

The **Crockpot** took the **Distressed Cook** aside just before she was plugged in to cook. "There are six things you need to know before you begin your fabulous meal in me."

First: **This is going to take longer to cook than a traditional oven or stove.**

Second: **You will be able to buy tougher and cheaper cuts of meat.**

Third: **You will have more flavor because the moisture will stay in.**

Fourth: **Every time you raise the lid you extend your cooking time by 30 minutes.**

Fifth: **You will not have a lot of dishes or a big mess to clean.**

Sixth: **If you will prepare your dinner in the morning you will have a stress free day with a fabulous meal to serve your family and friends.**

Now think of the Crockpot as **GOD** and **YOU** as the Distressed Cook.

First: This is going to take longer to cook than a traditional oven or stove.
Trust Me. Have Faith. Being a Believer takes a lifetime. It's a Journey not a Destination.

Second: You will be able to buy tougher and cheaper cuts of meat.
You will have tough times in your life but if you will be Obedient in MY word and ask ME for help I will make your heart tender.

Third: You will have more flavor because the moisture will stay in.
If you will keep ME in your heart I will season you with the Fruit of the Spirit.

Fourth: Every time you raise the lid you extend your cooking time by 30 minutes.
Don't try to do it without ME and do it by yourself. Keep ME inside.

Fifth: You will not have a lot of dishes or a big mess to clean.
No matter how big a mess your life may seem I will help you clean it up.

Sixth: If you will prepare your dinner in the morning you will have a stress free day with a fabulous meal to serve your family and friends.
If you begin your day spending time in MY WORD and PRAYER you will be able to SERVE others.

Debbie Thornton

Beef Stroganoff	Satisfy Off	131
SATISFACTION	**Romans 1:17**	132
BBQ Short Ribs	Don't Short His Word	133
REDUNDANT	**Romans 10:17**	134
Gravy Short Ribs	Smother Me With HIS Ribs	135
Honey Mustard BBQ Short Ribs	Honey I'm Not Short On Faith	135
HEAVEN	**Galatians 5:5**	136
Dijon Chuck Roast	Roasted Satan	137
SHIELD	**Ephesians 6:16**	138
Horseradish Chuck Roast	Horsing Around Faith	139
Lemon Pepper Chuck Roast	Don't Be Sour Get HIS Power	139
POWER	**Matthew 21:21**	140
Italian Rump Roast	Roasted With Obedience	141
RECEIVE	**James 2:14**	142
Asian Flank Steak	Flanked In Armour	143
Round Steak & Gravy	Pad Your Steak	143
REVEALED	**1 Thessalonians 5:8**	144
Herbed Round Steak	Rounded For Our Sins	145
Mexican Round Steak	Steak Out For Us	145
PRICE	**Hebrews 6:19**	146
Salsa Swiss Steak	Swiss Your Wish	147
Gravy Stew Meat	Stewing For HIS Will	147
WILL	**Hebrews 10:36**	148

"I know about GOD, but do I KNOW GOD?"

Cranberry Brisket
"Berried In Belief"

1   (2-3 pound) beef brisket
       salt & pepper, to taste
1   (16 ounce) can whole cranberry sauce
1   (8 ounce) can tomato sauce
1   onion, chopped
1   Tablespoon prepared mustard

RUB brisket with salt & pepper.
PLACE brisket in crockpot.
COMBINE last 4 ingredients in a bowl. STIR.
POUR over brisket. COVER.
COOK on LOW for 10 hours or HIGH for 5 hours.

Corned Beef Brisket & Cabbage
"Receive HIS Word"

2   onions, sliced
1   (2-3 pound) corned beef brisket
1   cup apple juice
$\frac{1}{4}$ cup brown sugar
2   teaspoons prepared mustard
6   whole cloves
6   cabbage wedges

PLACE onions in crockpot. PLACE brisket over onions.
COMBINE next 4 ingredients in a bowl. MIX well.
POUR over brisket. PLACE cabbage on top of brisket.
COVER.COOK on LOW for 10 hours or HIGH for 5 hours.

RECEIVE

As the body without the spirit is dead, so faith without deeds is dead.
James 2:26 (NIV)

BLONDE A.D.D. INTERPRETATION:

IT'S NOT ENOUGH JUST TO BELIEVE HIS WORD YOU HAVE TO RECEIVE

YOUR INTERPRETATION:

_____ _____ _____ _____ _____

_____ _____ _____ _____ _____

8 Layer Beef Dish
"Layer Your Focus"

1½	pounds lean ground beef, uncooked
4	Tablespoons bacon bits
1	onion, chopped
2	(8 ounce) cans tomato sauce
1	cup water
1	teaspoon chili powder
½	teaspoon salt
½	teaspoon pepper
1	cup long grain rice, uncooked
2	(15 ounce) cans whole kernel corn, drained
1	bell pepper, chopped

LAYER 1st 3 ingredients in order given in crockpot.
COMBINE next 5 ingredients in a bowl.
POUR ½ of tomato sauce mixture over beef.
SPRINKLE rice then corn over tomato mixture.
TOP with remaining tomato sauce, then bell pepper.
COVER. COOK on **LOW** for 8 hours or **HIGH** for 4 hours.

Chill

To refrigerate food; Not to be confused with when you are starting to get the flu, or to calm down.

HOPE

Let us hold unswervingly to the hope we profess, for he who promised is faithful.
Hebrews 10:23 (NIV)

BLONDE A.D.D. INTERPRETATION:

HOLD ON TO HOPE
WITH HIM YOU COPE

YOUR INTERPRETATION:

_____ _____ _____ _____

_____ _____ _____ _____

BBQ Beans & Beef
"Bean Focused"

2	pounds lean ground beef
1	onion, chopped
1	(8 ounce) can tomato sauce
½	cup picante sauce
2	Tablespoons balsamic vinegar
2	Tablespoons brown sugar
1	Tablespoon chili powder
2	teaspoons Worcestershire
¼	teaspoon pepper
2	garlic cloves, crushed
3	(16 ounce) cans kidney beans

BROWN beef & onion in a skillet. DRAIN.
POUR all ingredients in crockpot. STIR. COVER.
COOK on HIGH for 1 hour.
TURN setting on LOW. COOK for 5 hours.

Combine

To mix various ingredients together; Not to be confused with a harvester that heads and threshes and cleans grain.

FOCUS

Let us fix our eyes on Jesus, the author and perfecter of our faith, who for the joy set before him endured the cross, scorning its shame, and sat down at the right hand of the throne of God.
Hebrews 12:2 (NIV)

BLONDE A.D.D. INTERPRETATION:

FOCUS ON THE CROSS
YOU WON'T BE LOST

YOUR INTERPRETATION:

_____ _____ _____ _____

_____ _____ _____ _____

"I know about GOD, but do I KNOW GOD?"

Beef Cabbage Dish
"Refined Is Divine"

1	(16 ounce) bag shredded cabbage
1	pound lean ground beef, uncooked
1	teaspoon salt
1	teaspoon pepper
1	onion, chopped
1	cup long grain rice, uncooked
1	(28 ounce) jar chunky spaghetti sauce
$\frac{1}{2}$	cup water
$\frac{1}{4}$	teaspoon dried basil leaves
$\frac{1}{4}$	teaspoon seasoned salt

PLACE $\frac{1}{2}$ of cabbage in crockpot.
CRUMBLE beef over top of cabbage.
SPRINKLE salt & pepper over beef.
PUT onion & rice over beef.
TOP with remaining cabbage.
COMBINE last 4 ingredients in a bowl. **MIX** well.
POUR over cabbage. COVER.
COOK on LOW for 8 hours or HIGH for 4 hours.

Coat

To roll food in flour, nuts, sugar, crumbs, etc. until all sides are evenly covered; or to dip first into slightly beaten egg or milk, then to cover with whatever coating is called for in a recipe; Not to be confused with something you wear when you are cold.

REFINED

These have come so that your faith—of greater worth than gold, which perishes even though refined by fire—may be proved genuine and may result in praise, glory and honor when Jesus Christ is revealed.
1 Peter 1:7 (NIV)

BLONDE A.D.D. INTERPRETATION:

OUR TRIALS AND STRUGGLES WILL REFINE
HE PLANS AND DIRECTS; HE'S DIVINE

YOUR INTERPRETATION:

_____ _____ _____ _____ _____ _____

_____ _____ _____ _____ _____ _____

"I know about GOD, but do I KNOW GOD?"

Beef & Macaroni Dish
"Don't Act Noodled"

1	(8 ounce) macaroni, cooked
2	Tablespoons oil
1½	pounds lean ground beef, browned, drained
1	teaspoon salt
1	teaspoon pepper
1	onion, chopped
2	celery stalks, chopped
1	(8 ounce) can tomato paste
¾	cup water
2	Tablespoons sherry
1	can tomato soup
1	teaspoon dried oregano
2	cups shredded cheddar cheese

SPRAY crockpot with cooking spray.
TOSS macaroni in oil. PLACE in crockpot.
COMBINE next 10 ingredients in crockpot. MIX well.
COVER. COOK on LOW for 6 hours or HIGH for 3 hours.
SPRINKLE cheese over all ingredients.
HEAT on HIGH until cheese is melted.

Pinch
The amount of a ingredient you can hold between your thumb and forefinger... about 1/16 teaspoon; Not to be confused with what is done to someone on St. Patrick's Day.

ACT

We know that we have come to know him if we obey his commands.
1 John 2:3 (NIV)

BLONDE A.D.D. INTERPRETATION:

THE WAY WE ACT
IS THE PLAIN FACT

YOUR INTERPRETATION:

___ __ ____ __ ____

____ ____ ___ ____

"I know about GOD, but do I KNOW GOD?"

Beef & Potato Dish
"Dish Out Praise"

2	pounds lean ground beef
1	can tomato soup
¼	cup onion, chopped
	salt & pepper, to taste
6	potatoes, peeled, sliced
1	cup light cream

BROWN beef in a skillet. **DRAIN.**
COMBINE next 4 ingredients in a bowl.
LAYER potatoes & meat in crockpot.
POUR soup mixture over meat/potatoes. **COVER.**
COOK on **LOW** for 6 hours or **HIGH** for 3 hours.
TURN control on **HIGH. POUR** cream over mixture.
COVER. COOK on **HIGH** for 20 minutes.

Beef Stuffed Squash
"Squashy About Our Gift"

1	pound lean ground beef
1	cup onion, chopped
1	bell pepper, chopped
1	teaspoon salt
1	cup shredded cheddar cheese, divided
2	squash, cut lengthwise, inside scooped out

BROWN 1st 3 ingredients in a skillet. **DRAIN.**
ADD salt & cheese. **FILL** squash with meat mixture.
PLACE squash in crockpot. **COVER.COOK** on **LOW** for 4 hours.

GIFT

For it is by grace you have been saved, through faith—and this not from yourselves, it is the gift of God.
Ephesians 2:8 (NIV)

BLONDE A.D.D. INTERPRETATION:

OUR GIFT WE SHOULD ENJOY
GIVE HIM GRATITUDE, PRAISE, JOY

YOUR INTERPRETATION:

_____ _____ _____ _____ _____

_____ _____ _____ _____

BBQ Meatloaf
"Don't Loaf In Your Belief"

2	pounds lean ground beef
1	can tomato soup, divided
1	egg, beaten
1	cup crackers, crushed
2	Tablespoons honey
2	teaspoons Worcestershire, divided
2	Tablespoons dried minced onions
$\frac{1}{2}$	teaspoon salt
$\frac{1}{4}$	teaspoon pepper
$\frac{1}{2}$	cup water
2	teaspoons prepared mustard
2	Tablespoons brown sugar

COMBINE 1st 9 ingredients in a bowl. MIX well.
FORM in a oblong shape.
PLACE foil in crockpot with ends extending out.
PLACE meat in crockpot. COMBINE last 3 ingredients.
MIX well. POUR over meat. COVER.
COOK on LOW for 10 hours or HIGH for 5 hours

Mix

To stir, usually with a spoon, until all ingredients are thoroughly combined; Not to be confused with company that is mixed (whatever that means)

CONCEIVE

We live by faith, not by sight.
2 Corinthians 5:7 (NIV)

BLONDE A.D.D INTERPRETATION:

YOU WILL CONCEIVE
IF YOU BELIEVE

YOUR INTERPRETATION:

_____ _____ _____

_____ _____ _____

"I know about GOD, but do I KNOW GOD?"

Meatloaf
"Don't Loaf In Your Faith"

1 ½	pounds lean ground beef
1	egg, beaten
1	cup onion, chopped
1	cup bread crumbs
2	teaspoons prepared mustard
1	teaspoon Worcestershire
1	teaspoon dried parsley flakes
1	cup ketchup, divided ½ cup

COMBINE all ingredients in a large bowl.
SHAPE meat in a round shape.
PLACE meat mixture in cooking sprayed crockpot.
POUR divided ½ cup ketchup over meat. COVER.
COOK on LOW for 8 hours or HIGH for 4 hours.

Stuffed Bell Peppers
"Stuffed Faith"

1½	pounds lean ground beef
1	cup onion, chopped
1	teaspoon salt
½	cup long grain rice, cooked
4	bell peppers, tops cut off, seeds removed
1	(8 ounce) can tomato sauce

BROWN 1st 2 ingredients. DRAIN. ADD salt & rice to meat.
FILL bell peppers with meat mixture. PLACE peppers in crockpot.
SPOON remaining meat over peppers. POUR sauce over peppers.
COVER. COOK on LOW for 4 hours or HIGH for 2 hours.

BELIEVE

Now faith is being sure of what we hope for and certain of what we do not see.
Hebrews 11:1 (NIV)

BLONDE A.D.D INTERPRETATION:

ASSURANCE OF A FUTURE REALITY IF WE DON'T BELIEVE...FATALITY

YOUR INTERPRETATION:

_____ _____ _____ _____ _____

_____ _____ _____ _____ _____

"I know about GOD, but do I KNOW GOD?"

Spaghetti Sauce
"Possibly Saucy"

2	pounds lean ground beef
1	onion, chopped
1	bell pepper, chopped
2	celery stalks, chopped
1	garlic clove, crushed
1	Tablespoon Italian seasoning
1	(28 ounce) can stewed tomatoes
1	(8 ounce) can tomato paste
1	(16 ounce) can tomato sauce
2	cups water
1	envelope dry spaghetti seasoning mix
	salt & pepper, to taste

BROWN 1st 5 ingredients in a skillet. DRAIN.
COMBINE all ingredients in crockpot. MIX well.
COVER. COOK on HIGH until sauce comes to a boil.
COOK on LOW for 6 hours or HIGH for 3 hours.
SERVE over noodles.

Dot

To scatter small amounts of specified ingredients, usually butter, nuts or chocolate on top of food; Not to be confused with my Aunt Dorothy or my husband's Mother.

POSSIBLE

He replied, "Because you have so little faith. I tell you the truth, if you have faith as small as a mustard seed, you can say to this mountain, 'Move from here to there' and it will move. Nothing will be impossible for you."
Matthew 17:20 (NIV)

BLONDE A.D.D INTERPRETATION:

WITHOUT GOD IT'S IMPOSSIBLE WITH GOD IT'S POSSIBLE

YOUR INTERPRETATION:

_____ _____ _____ _____

_____ _____ _____ _____

Beef Stroganoff
"Satisfy Off"

2	pounds lean ground beef
1	onion, chopped
1	garlic clove, crushed
3	teaspoons salt
2	teaspoons pepper
1	(4 ounce) jar sliced mushrooms, drained
3	Tablespoons tomato paste
1	cup beef broth
1½	cups sour cream, with 4 Tablespoons flour
1	(8 ounce) noodles, cooked

BROWN 1st 3 ingredients in a skillet. **DRAIN.**
POUR in crockpot. **ADD** next 5 ingredients. **MIX** well.
COVER.COOK on **LOW** for 6 hours or **HIGH** for 3 hours.
ADD sour cream & flour last hour of cooking. **STIR.**
SERVE over noodles.

Dice

To cut food into small cubes of uniform size and shape, usually about ¼ inch in size; Not to be confused with a cube with 6 different faces.

SATISFACTION

For in the gospel a righteousness from God is revealed, a righteousness that is by faith from first to last, just as it is written: "The righteous will live by faith."
Romans 1:17 (NIV)

BLONDE A.D.D INTERPRETATION:

FAITH SHOWS THROUGH ACTIONS THIS IS GOD'S SATISFACTION

YOUR INTERPRETATION:

____ ____ ____ ____

____ ____ ____ ____

"I know about GOD, but do I KNOW GOD?"

BBQ Short Ribs
"Don't Short His Word"

4	pounds beef country short ribs
1	Tablespoon oil
1	onion, cut in wedges
1	cup water
¼	cup balsamic vinegar
1	Tablespoon paprika
1	teaspoon curry powder
½	teaspoon chili powder
½	teaspoon dry mustard
2	teaspoons salt
1	Tablespoon cornstarch
2	Tablespoons water

BROWN 1st 2 ingredients in a skillet.
COMBINE all ingredients in crockpot. COVER.
COOK on LOW for 8 hours or HIGH for 4 hours.

Pound
To flatten meats and chicken (which I call a meat) to a uniform thickness using a meat mallet; Not to be confused with where stray dogs are put, or basic units of money in Great Britain (Can ya believe I knew that?)

REDUNDANT

Consequently, faith comes from hearing the message, and the message is heard through the word of Christ.
Romans 10:17 (NIV)

BLONDE A.D.D INTERPRETATION:

WHEN YOU ARE REDUNDANT FAITH IS SO ABUNDANT

YOUR INTERPRETATION:

_____ _____ _____ _____

_____ _____ _____ _____

Gravy Short Ribs
"Smother Me With HIS Ribs"

4	pounds beef short ribs
1	teaspoon pepper
1	(12 ounce) jar beef gravy
1	(16 ounce) frozen stir-fry bell peppers & onions

PLACE ribs in crockpot. SPRINKLE with PEPPER.
POUR gravy over ribs. COVER.
COOK on LOW for 10 hours or HIGH for 5 hours.
SKIM fat from top of liquid in crockpot. REMOVE ribs.
ADD bell peppers & onions to crockpot. COVER.
COOK on HIGH for 30 minutes.
SERVE vegetables & sauce over ribs.

Honey Mustard BBQ Short Ribs
"Honey I'm Not Short On Faith"

3	pounds beef short ribs
½	cup Dijon mustard
1	garlic clove, crushed
2	Tablespoons honey
½	teaspoon salt
½	teaspoon pepper
1	cup barbecue sauce

PLACE short ribs in crockpot.
COMBINE last 6 ingredients in a bowl. POUR over ribs.
COVER. COOK on LOW for 8 hours or HIGH for 4 hours.

HEAVEN

But by faith we eagerly await through the Spirit the righteousness for which we hope.
Galatians 5:5 (NIV)

BLONDE A.D.D INTERPRETATION:

BECAUSE THE BIBLE TELLS ME SO I KNOW WHERE I WILL GO

YOUR INTERPRETATION:

_____ _____ _____ _____ _____ _____

_____ _____ _____ _____ _____ _____

"I know about GOD, but do I KNOW GOD?"

Dijon Chuck Roast
"Roasted Satan"

1	(3-4 pound) boneless chuck roast
1	onion, chopped
$\frac{1}{4}$	cup water
4	dried shiitake mushrooms, rinsed
$\frac{1}{4}$	cup ketchup
$\frac{1}{4}$	cup red wine
$\frac{1}{2}$	cup Dijon mustard
1	Tablespoon Worcestershire
$\frac{1}{2}$	teaspoon salt
$\frac{1}{2}$	teaspoon pepper
1	garlic clove, crushed
2	Tablespoons cornstarch
3	Tablespoons water

PLACE roast and onion in crockpot.
COMBINE next 9 ingredients in a bowl.
POUR mixture over roast. COVER.
COOK on LOW for 10 hours or HIGH for 5 hours.
REMOVE roast. SLICE. KEEP meat warm.
TURN crockpot on HIGH.
DISSOLVE cornstarch in water.
STIR. COVER. COOK on HIGH for 25 minutes.
SERVE juices over roast.

Reduce
To evaporate some of the liquid in stock or sauce by boiling; Not to be confused with losing weight or subtract.

SHIELD

In addition to all this, take up the shield of faith, with which you can extinguish all the flaming arrows of the evil one.
Ephesians 6:16 (NIV)

BLONDE A.D.D. INTERPRETATION:

WHEN YOU TRUST IN GOD YOU HAVE A SHIELD
FROM THE LIES AND PROMISES OF PLEASURE SATAN REVEALS

YOUR INTERPRETATION:

___ ___ ___ ___ ___ ___ ___ ___ ___ ___

___ ___ ___ ___ ___ ___ ___ ___ ___ ___

"I know about GOD, but do I KNOW GOD?"

Horseradish Chuck Roast
"Horsing Around Faith"

1	(3-4 pound) boneless chuck roast
1	Tablespoon oil
8	potatoes, peeled, cut in half
1	(16 ounce) bag baby carrots
1	onion, chopped
1	(5 ounce) jar prepared horseradish
1	teaspoon salt
½	teaspoon pepper
1	cup water

BROWN 1st 2 ingredients in a large skillet.
PLACE next 3 ingredients in crockpot.
PUT roast over vegetables. COMBINE next 3 ingredients.
SPREAD evenly over roast. POUR water over roast.
COVER.COOK on LOW for 10 hours or HIGH for 5½ hours.

Lemon Pepper Chuck Roast
"Don't Be Sour Get HIS Power"

1	(2-3 pound) chuck roast
½	teaspoon seasoned salt
½	teaspoon lemon pepper
¼	teaspoon paprika
1	cup beef broth

RUB roast with salt, pepper & paprika.
PLACE roast in crockpot. ADD broth. COVER.
COOK on LOW for 8 hours or HIGH for 4 hours.

POWER

Jesus replied, "I tell you the truth, if you have faith and do not doubt, not only can you do what was done to the fig tree, but also you can say to this mountain, 'Go, throw yourself into the sea,' and it will be done."
Matthew 21:21 (NIV)

BLONDE A.D.D. INTERPRETATION:

WHEN YOU HAVE FAITH AND LIVE IMMEASURABLE POWER IS WHAT HE GIVES

YOUR INTERPRETATION:

_____ _____ _____ _____ _____ _____

_____ _____ _____ _____ _____

"I know about GOD, but do I KNOW GOD?"

Italian Rump Roast
"Roasted With Obedience"

1	(3-4 pound) rump roast
1	(8 ounce) can tomato sauce
2½	cups water
1	teaspoon salt
1	teaspoon pepper
1	teaspoon parsley flakes
1	teaspoon garlic powder
1	teaspoon basil
1	teaspoon oregano
1	teaspoon Worcestershire
1	teaspoon soy sauce
2	envelopes dry Italian seasoning mix

PLACE roast in crockpot.
COMBINE next 11 ingredients in a bowl.
MIX well.
POUR over roast. COVER.
COOK on LOW for 10 hours or HIGH for 5 hours.

Peel

To strip or slip off outer coverings of fruits or vegetables; Not to be confused with making a screeching sound with your car.

RECEIVE

What good is it, my brothers, if a man claims to have faith but has no deeds? Can such faith save him?
James 2:14 (NIV)

BLONDE A.D.D INTERPRETATION:

JUST BECAUSE YOU SAY YOU BELIEVE DOESN'T MEAN THAT YOU REALLY RECEIVE

YOUR INTERPRETATION:

_____ ____ ____ ____ ____ ____

_____ ____ ____ ____ ____ ____

Asian Flank Steak
"Flanked In Armour"

2	pounds flank steak, cut in 6 pieces
2	Tablespoons oil
6	slices pineapple rings in juice, reserve $\frac{1}{2}$ cup juice
2	Tablespoons soy sauce
1	teaspoon ginger
1	Tablespoon sherry
2	Tablespoons brown sugar
1	teaspoon Worcestershire
	salt & pepper, to taste

BROWN steak in hot oil on all sides in a large skillet.
PLACE steak in crockpot. PLACE pineapple rings on steak.
COMBINE last 7 ingredients in a bowl. MIX well.
POUR over steak. COVER.
COOK on LOW for 8 hours or HIGH for 4 hours.

Round Steak & Gravy
"Pad Your Steak"

2	pounds boneless round steak, cut in 6 pieces
2	Tablespoons oil
1	(16 ounce) can beef broth
2	envelopes dry brown gravy mix
1	envelope dry onion soup mix
$\frac{1}{2}$	cup water

BROWN steak in hot oil in a skillet. PUT in crockpot.
COMBINE last 4 ingredients in a bowl. MIX well.
POUR broth mixture over steak. COVER.
COOK on LOW for 8 hours or HIGH for 4 hours.

REVEALED

But since we belong to the day, let us be self-controlled, putting on faith and love as a breastplate, and the hope of salvation as a helmet.
1 Thessalonians 5:8 (NIV)

BLONDE A.D.D. INTERPRETATION:

HAVING FAITH AND LOVE AS OUR SHIELD
IS THE HOPE OF SALVATION THAT'S REVEALED

YOUR INTERPRETATION:

____ ___ ___ ___ ___ ___ ___ ___

____ ___ ___ ___ ___ ___ ___

"I know about GOD, but do I KNOW GOD?"

Herbed Round Steak
"Rounded For Our Sins"

2	pounds round steak, cut in 6 pieces
1	Tablespoon oil
1	onion, sliced, separate rings
1	can of cream of celery soup
1	teaspoon oregano
½	teaspoon thyme
1	Tablespoon garlic powder
1	Tablespoon Worcestershire
	salt & pepper, to taste

BROWN steak in hot oil in a skillet.
PLACE onions in crockpot. PUT steak on top of onions.
COMBINE last 7 ingredients in a bowl. MIX well.
POUR over steak. COVER.
COOK on LOW for 8 hours or HIGH for 4 hours.

Mexican Round Steak
"Steak Out For Us"

2	pounds round steak, cut in 6 pieces
1	(10 ounce) bag frozen whole kernal corn
1	(18 ounce) jar chunky salsa
1	(14 ounce) can black beans, rinsed, drained
1	onion, chopped
½	cup water

PLACE steak in crockpot.
COMBINE last 5 ingredients in a bowl. MIX well.
POUR over steak. COVER.
COOK on LOW for 8 hours or HIGH for 4 hours.

"I know about GOD, but do I KNOW GOD?"

PRICE

We have this hope as an anchor for the soul, firm and secure. It enters the inner sanctuary behind the curtain,
Hebrews 6:19 (NIV)

BLONDE A.D.D INTERPRETATION:

OUR HOPE IS IN CHRIST
HE ENTERED FOR OUR PRICE

YOUR INTERPRETATION:

_____ _____ _____ _____

_____ _____ _____ _____

"I know about GOD, but do I KNOW GOD?"

Salsa Swiss Steak
"Swiss Your Wish"

2	pounds swiss steak, cut in 5 pieces
1	teaspoon salt
1	teaspoon pepper
1	Tablespoon oil
2	onions, sliced, separated in rings
1	can cream of mushroom soup
2	cups thick & chunky salsa

BROWN salt & peppered steak in hot oil.
PLACE steak in crockpot. TOP with onions.
COMBINE last 2 ingredients in skillet with steak drippings.
POUR over steak. COVER.
COOK on LOW for 8 hours or HIGH for 4 hours.

Gravy Stew Meat
"Stewing For HIS Will"

2	pounds beef stew meat, cut in cubes
4	Tablespoons oil
1	can cream of celery soup
1	can cream of mushroom soup
2	cups water
2	Tablespoons Worcestershire
2	Tablespoons soy sauce

BROWN meat in hot oil in a skillet. PUT meat in crockpot.
COMBINE last 5 ingredients in a bowl.
POUR soup mixture over beef in crockpot. MIX well.
COVER. COOK on LOW for 8 hours or HIGH for 4 hours.

WILL

You need to persevere so that when you have done the will of God, you will receive what he has promised.
Hebrews 10:36 (NIV)

BLONDE A.D.D. INTERPRETATION:

LIVE DAILY IN HIS WILL
YOU WILL HAVE A THRILL

YOUR INTERPRETATION:

_____ _____ _____ _____

_____ _____ _____ _____

CHICKEN

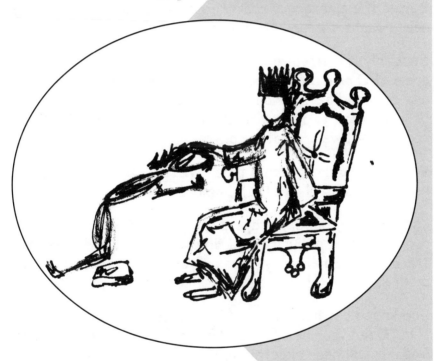

PRAYER

Prayer

As I sit here this evening thinking about what to write about prayer, the words of profundity leave me. Perhaps it is because I am exhausted after spending part of the weekend in the emergency room with my precious Mother.

Spending time in an emergency room has a way of cutting through the sweet, pink, fluffy, cotton-candy of platitudes. During the emergency room times of our lives our priorities are brought sharply into focus.

Suddenly it matters not what kind of car we drive or if we are a CEO or a ditch-digger. All that matters is the safety and care and help for our loved ones. Suddenly we are brought face-to-face with our vulnerability and with the reality that we are not in control.

What do you do in such a time? We go to the One who we know is in control and that One is God.

Long-winded, flowery prayers aren't found in emergency rooms. (God isn't impressed with all of our words, He hears the heart). Emergency room prayers are short and to the point such as HELP; Thank you; Please; Guide Me, Save Us.

God knows our hearts and He wants us to be honest with Him. Open your heart to God and pray your heart words to God. He will hear exactly what you are trying to say.

Father, thank you for hearing our prayers. Draw close to us as we draw close to you. Amen.

Ginger Williamson

Apricot Chicken
"Be A Selfless Chick"

6   boneless, skinless chicken breasts
2   cups apricot preserves
2   Tablespoons prepared mustard
3   teaspoons Worcestershire
     salt & pepper, to taste

PLACE chicken in cooking sprayed crockpot.
COMBINE last 5 ingredients in a bowl. MIX well.
SPOON over chicken. COVER.
COOK on LOW for 8 hours or HIGH for 4 hours.

Artichoke Chicken
"Choking For Selflessness"

6   boneless, skinless chicken breasts, cut in strips
1   Tablespoon real bacon bits
1   (15 ounce) can diced tomatoes, drained
1   (15 ounce) can artichoke hearts, quartered
1   (8 ounce) fresh mushrooms, sliced
1   envelope dry chicken gravy mix
$\frac{1}{4}$ cup red wine
2   Tablespoons Dijon mustard

COMBINE all ingredients in crockpot. MIX well.
COVER.COOK on LOW for 8 hours or HIGH for 4 hours.
SERVE over rice or noodles.

SELFLESS

Then he said to them all: "If anyone would come after me, he must deny himself and take up his cross daily and follow me."
Luke 9:23 (NIV)

BLONDE A.D.D. INTERPRETATION:

PUT ASIDE SELFISH DESIRES AND YOU WILL ACQUIRE

YOUR INTERPRETATION:

_____ _____ _____ _____

_____ _____ _____ _____

Basil Chicken
"Hey Chick, Call"

6	boneless, skinless chicken breasts
1	teaspoon pepper
½	cup basil pesto
2	cans cream of celery soup
1	bell pepper, chopped

PLACE chicken in crockpot. COMBINE next 3 ingredients.
SPOON soup mixture over chicken.
SPRINKLE bell pepper over soup & chicken. COVER.
COOK on LOW for 8 hours or HIGH for 4 hours.

Black Bean Salsa Chicken
"Bean Calling A Long Time"

1	(15 ounce) can black beans, rinsed, drained
2	(15 ounce) cans whole kernel corn, drained
2	cups salsa, divided 1 cup
6	boneless, skinless chicken breasts
1	cup shredded cheddar cheese

COMBINE 1st 2 ingredients with 1 cup salsa. MIX well.
POUR black bean mixture in crockpot.
PLACE chicken over mixture.
POUR remaining salsa over chicken.
COVER. COOK on LOW for 8 hours or HIGH for 4 hours.
SPRINKLE cheese over chicken. COOK 15 minutes on HIGH.

CONFESSING

If we confess our sins, he is faithful and just and will forgive us our sins and purify us from all unrighteousness.
1 John 1:9 (NIV)

BLONDE A.D.D INTERPRETATION:

GOD CLEANSES THOSE WHO ARE CONFESSING
BEING FORGIVEN IS SUCH A BLESSING

YOUR INTERPRETATION:

_____ _____ _____ _____ _____

_____ _____ _____ _____ _____

Brandy Chicken
"Obedient Chick"

2	Tablespoons oil
1	Tablespoon margarine
	salt & pepper, to taste
1	teaspoon dried oregano
6	boneless, skinless chicken breasts
$\frac{1}{4}$	cup white wine
$\frac{1}{2}$	cup brandy
$\frac{1}{4}$	cup cream

BROWN chicken in 1st 5 ingredients in a skillet.
PLACE chicken in crockpot.
POUR wine & brandy in skillet chicken was browned in.
BOIL. POUR in crockpot. COVER.
COOK on LOW for 8 hours or HIGH for 4 hours.
PUSH chicken aside in crockpot. POUR in cream. STIR.
SERVE over pasta.

Broccoli Chicken
"Cluck Cluck For Obedience"

3	carrots, sliced
1	head of broccoli, cut in 2-inch pieces
6	boneless, skinless chicken breasts
2	cans cream of mushroom soup

PLACE 1st 2 ingredients in crockpot.
LAY chicken over broccoli and carrots.
POUR soup over chicken. COVER.
COOK on LOW for 8 hours or HIGH for 4 hours.

STRENGTHEN

I prayed to the LORD my God and confessed: "O Lord, the great and awesome God, who keeps his covenant of love with all who love him and obey his commands,"
Daniel 9:4 (NIV)

BLONDE A.D.D INTERPRETATION:

STRENGTHEN BY CONFESSION WHAT A LESSON

YOUR INTERPRETATION:

_____ _____ _____

_____ _____ _____

Brown Sugar Chicken
"Sugar Coated Wrongs"

4	boneless, skinless chicken breasts
1	cup brown sugar
½	cup balsamic vinegar
½	cup lemon lime soda
3	Tablespoons minced garlic
2	Tablespoons soy sauce
	salt & pepper, to taste

PLACE chicken in crockpot.
COMBINE last 7 ingredients in a bowl.
MIX well. POUR over chicken. COVER.
COOK on LOW for 8 hour or HIGH for 4 hours.
SERVE over rice or noodles.

Southwestern Chicken
"Belonging Chick"

4	boneless, skinless chicken breasts
1	Tablespoon chili powder
1	(14 ounce) can chunky tomatoes
1	(15 ounce) can black beans, rinsed, drained
1	(11 ounce) can Mexi-Corn, drained

PLACE chicken in crockpot.
COMBINE last 4 ingredients. MIX well.
SPOON mixture over chicken. COVER.
COOK on LOW for 8 hours or HIGH for 4 hours.

WRONG

They said, "Turn now, each of you, from your evil ways and your evil practices, and you can stay in the land the LORD gave to you and your fathers for ever and ever."
Jeremiah 25:5 (NIV)

BLONDE A.D.D. INTERPRETATION:

CONFESS WHAT YOU DID WRONG HE WILL MAKE YOU STRONG

YOUR INTERPRETATION:

_____ _____ _____ _____ _____

_____ _____ _____ _____ _____

Cajun Chicken
"My Past Cajun Chick"

2   Tablespoons margarine
1   bell pepper, chopped
1   onion, chopped
2   celery stalks, chopped
6   boneless, skinless chicken breasts
4   teaspoons Creole seasoning
1   (14 ounce) can diced tomatoes
2   cups rice, cooked

BROWN chicken with 1st 4 ingredients in a skillet.
SPRINKLE chicken with Creole seasoning while cooking.
POUR chicken & vegetable mixture in crockpot.
POUR tomatoes over chicken. **STIR.**
COVER. COOK on **LOW** for 8 hours or **HIGH** for 4 hours.
SERVE over rice.

Chicken Chili
"Chili About My Past"

2   pounds boneless, skinless chicken thighs
3   (14 ounce) cans diced tomatoes with chilies & garlic
1   envelope dry taco seasoning mix
2   (15 ounce) cans white beans, drained, rinsed

COMBINE all ingredients in crockpot. **COVER.**
COOK on **LOW** for 8 hours or **HIGH** on 4 hours.

PAST

We have sinned and done wrong. We have been wicked and have rebelled; we have turned away from your commands and laws.
Daniel 9:5 (NIV)

BLONDE A.D.D INTERPRETATION:

DON'T LET YOUR PAST SINS MAKE YOU NOT GET IN

YOUR INTERPRETATION:

_____ _____ _____ _____ _____

_____ _____ _____ _____ _____

Coca-Cola Chicken
"Troubled Chick"

6	boneless, skinless chicken breasts
1	onion, chopped
1	(12 ounce) can coca-cola
1	(8 ounce) bottle ketchup
3	Tablespoons brown sugar
1	teaspoon salt
1	teaspoon pepper

LAYER all ingredients in crockpot in order given.
STIR 1 time. COVER.
COOK on LOW for 8 hours or HIGH for 4 hours.

Chicken Cordon Bleu
"Bleu Chick"

6	boneless, skinless chicken breasts
6	Swiss cheese slices
2	cans cream of mushroom soup
3	Tablespoons water
$\frac{1}{4}$	teaspoon pepper
$\frac{1}{2}$	teaspoon salt

FLATTEN each breast with a mallet.
PLACE piece of cheese in center of each breast.
ROLL UP. SECURE with toothpick.
PUT chicken in crockpot.
COMBINE last 4 ingredients. POUR over chicken.
COVER. COOK on LOW for 8 hours or HIGH for 4 hours.

TROUBLES

Just as it is written in the Law of Moses, all this disaster has come upon us, yet we have not sought the favor of the LORD our God by turning from our sins and giving attention to your truth. Daniel 9:13 (NIV)

BLONDE A.D.D. INTERPRETATION:

HELP ME THROUGH MY TROUBLES SO MY TROUBLES WON'T DOUBLE

YOUR INTERPRETATION:

____ ____ ____ ____ ____

____ ____ ____ ____ ____

Cranberry Chicken
"Berry My Sin Chick"

1	(16 ounce) can whole cranberry sauce
1	(8 ounce) French dressing
1	envelope dry onion soup mix
6	boneless, skinless chicken breasts

SPRAY crockpot with cooking spray.
COMBINE 1st 3 ingredients in crockpot. ADD breasts.
STIR to coat breasts. COVER.
COOK on LOW for 8 hours or HIGH for 4 hours.

Cranberry Apple Chicken
"Berried Mercy Chick"

6	boneless, skinless chicken breasts
1	(16 ounce) can whole cranberry sauce
1	Golden Delicious apple, chopped
1	teaspoon curry powder
$\frac{1}{2}$	cup pecans, chopped
$\frac{1}{2}$	cup flaked coconut

PUT chicken in crockpot. COMBINE next 3 ingredients.
POUR over chicken. COVER.
COOK on LOW for 8 hours or HIGH for 4 hours.
STIR in last 2 ingredients.

MERCY

Give ear, O God, and hear; open your eyes and see the desolation of the city that bears your Name. We do not make requests of you because we are righteous, but because of your great mercy.
Daniel 9:18 (NIV)

BLONDE A.D.D. INTERPRETATION:

YOU KNOW WE SINNED
BUT YOU CAME IN

YOUR INTERPRETATION:

_____ _____ _____ _____

_____ _____ _____ _____

Fruit Cocktail Chicken
"Rest In HIS Fruit"

1	(3-4 pound) whole roasting chicken, washed
1	Tablespoon salt
1	Tablespoon garlic powder
4	teaspoons soy sauce
1	(17 ounce) can chunky mixed fruit, drained
1	(10 ounce) jar sweet & sour sauce

SPRINKLE chicken with salt & garlic powder.
PLACE chicken in crockpot.
POUR soy sauce over chicken.
COOK on LOW for 8 hours or HIGH for 4 hours.
(1 hour before chicken is ready remove all but ½ cup broth)
POUR last 2 ingredients over chicken. COVER.
COOK on LOW for 1 hour or HIGH for 30 minutes.

Hot & Sour Chicken
"Sour Chick"

6	boneless, skinless chicken breasts
1	(14 ounce) can chicken broth
1	package Knorr's Hot & Sour Soup Mix

COMBINE all ingredients in crockpot. COVER.
COOK on LOW for 8 hours or HIGH for 4 hours.
SERVE over rice or noodles.

REST

"Come to me, all you who are weary and burdened, and I will give you rest."
Matthew 11:28 (NIV)

BLONDE A.D.D INTERPRETATION:

HIS REST IS LOVE, HEALING, PEACE
YOUR SIN, BURDEN, PERSECUTION WILL DECREASE

YOUR INTERPRETATION:

____ ____ ____ ____ ____ ____

____ ____ ____ ____ ____ ____

Green Chilies Stuffed Chicken
"Stuffed Sin"

1	(8 ounce) cream cheese, cubed
1	cup shredded cheddar cheese
1	(4 ounce) can diced green chilies
½	teaspoon chili powder
1	teaspoon salt
1	teaspoon pepper
4	boneless, skinless chicken breasts, pounded
1	can cream of mushroom soup
1	(10 ounce) can hot enchilada sauce

COMBINE 1st 6 ingredients in a bowl.
PLACE a Tablespoon of cheese mixture in each breast.
ROLL UP. SECURE with a toothpick.
PLACE chicken rolls in crockpot. (Seam side down)
POUR last 2 ingredients over chicken.
COVER.COOK on LOW for 8 hours or HIGH for 4 hours.

Saute'

To fry lightly until golden and tender in a small amount of oil on a stove, turning frequently; Not to be confused with the French word "To Jump".(See you not only are learning how to cook but you are learning French too)

CHICKEN
(Prayer)

WIN

Then I acknowledged my sin to you and did not cover up my iniquity. I said, "I will confess my transgressions to the LORD" and you forgave the guilt of my sin.
Psalm 32:5 (NIV)

BLONDE A.D.D. INTERPRETATION:

GETTING RID OF SIN
FOLLOWING GOD TO WIN

YOUR INTERPRETATION:

____ ____ ____ ____

____ ____ ____ ____

Creamy Italian Chicken
"Obedient Chick"

6	boneless, skinless chicken breasts, cut in strips
¼	cup margarine, melted
1	(8 ounce) cream cheese & chives, softened
1	can golden cream of mushroom soup
2	envelopes dry Italian dressing mix
1	cup water

COMBINE all ingredients in crockpot. STIR. COVER.
COOK on LOW for 8 hours or HIGH for 4 hours.
STIR. SERVE over rice or pasta.

Italian Chicken
"Laid Down HIS Lift"

6	boneless, skinless chicken breasts
¼	cup Italian seasoning
1	(8 ounce) fresh sliced mushrooms
1	(15 ounce) can tomato sauce
¼	cup red wine

PLACE chicken in cooking sprayed crockpot.
SPRINKLE with Italian seasoning.
PUT mushrooms on top of chicken.
POUR last 2 ingredients over chicken. COVER.
COOK on LOW for 8 hours or HIGH for 4 hours.
SERVE over rice.

FORGIVENESS

Jesus said, "Father, forgive them, for they do not know what they are doing." And they divided up his clothes by casting lots.
Luke 23:34 (NIV)

BLONDE A.D.D. INTERPRETATION:

GOD GAVE US A NEW LIFE THROUGH HIS SON
NOW LIVE IN HIS WORD AND OBEDIENCE IT'S FUN

YOUR INTERPRETATION:

___ ___ ___ ___ ___ ___ ___ ___ ___ ___

___ ___ ___ ___ ___ ___ ___ ___ ___ ___

Olive Chicken
"O Live"

6	boneless, skinless chicken breasts
½	cup wine (red or white)
¼	cup olive oil
¼	cup balsamic vinegar
2	Tablespoons oregano
2	bay leaves
4	garlic cloves, crushed
1	teaspoon pepper
1	teaspoon salt
3	Tablespoons capers, with a little juice
¾	cup green olives
¼	cup brown sugar

PLACE chicken in crockpot.
COMBINE last 11 ingredients in a bowl. MIX well.
POUR mixture over chicken. COVER.
COOK on LOW for 8 hours or HIGH for 4 hours.

Simmer

To cook in a liquid that is kept below boiling point; Not to be confused with what you have to do when you are really mad. Simmer Down.

PAST

Remember not the sins of my youth and my rebellious ways; according to your love remember me, for you are good, O LORD.
Psalm 25:7 (NIV)

BLONDE A.D.D. INTERPRETATION:

ALL THE SINS I DID IN THE PAST
I KNOW YOU WON'T LET THE PAIN LAST

YOUR INTERPRETATION:

___ ___ ___ ___ ___ ___ ___ ___ ___ ___

___ ___ ___ ___ ___ ___ ___ ___ ___ ___

French Onion Chicken
"Not A Regretful Chick"

4	boneless, skinless chicken breasts
1	(8 ounce) bottle French dressing
1	envelope dry onion soup mix
1	teaspoon salt
1	teaspoon pepper
1	(15 ounce) can whole cranberry sauce

PLACE chicken in crockpot.
COMBINE last 5 ingredients in a bowl. **MIX** well.
POUR mixture over chicken. **COVER.**
COOK on **LOW** for 8 hours or **HIGH** for 4 hours.

Orange Juice Chicken
"Juiced Out Regrets"

6	boneless, skinless chicken breasts
½	teaspoon ginger
1	teaspoon salt
1	teaspoon pepper
1	(6 ounce) can orange juice
2	cups rice, cooked
1½	cups shredded coconut
1	(11 ounce) can mandarin oranges
2	green onions, chopped

COMBINE 1st 5 ingredients in crockpot. **COVER.**
COOK on **LOW** for 8 hours or **HIGH** for 4 hours.
SERVE chicken over rice. **TOP** with last 3 ingredients.

REGRETS

"I, even I, am he who blots out your transgressions, for my own sake, and remembers your sins no more.
Isaiah 43:25 (NIV)

BLONDE A.D.D INTERPRETATION:

HE TOTALLY FORGETS
DON'T HAVE REGRETS

YOUR INTERPRETATION:

_____ _____ _____

_____ _____ _____

Peach Salsa Chicken
"Peachy & Salsy Receiver"

6   boneless, skinless chicken breasts
1   (16 ounce) jar peach salsa
1   teaspoon salt
1   teaspoon pepper

COMBINE all ingredients in crockpot. COVER.
COOK on LOW for 8 hours or HIGH for 4 hours.
SERVE over rice.

Pepper Jack Chicken
"Peppered Receiver"

6   boneless, skinless chicken breasts
2   bell peppers, cut in strips
1   can Pepper Jack cheese soup
1   cup chunky salsa

COMBINE all ingredients in crockpot. COVER.
COOK on LOW for 8 hours or HIGH for 4 hours.
SERVE over rice.

RECEIVE

All the prophets testify about him that everyone who believes in him receives forgiveness of sins through his name.
Acts 10:43 (NIV)

BLONDE A.D.D. INTERPRETATION:

WHEN WE REALLY BELIEVE FORGIVENESS WE WILL RECEIVE

YOUR INTERPRETATION:

___ ___ ___ ___

___ ___ ___ ___

Shrimp & Chicken Pasta
"Don't Hold A Grudge"

2	onions, chopped
3	garlic cloves, crushed
6	boneless, skinless chicken breasts, cut in chunks
1	(14 ounce) can diced tomatoes
2	Tablespoons tomato paste
1	(14 ounce) can chicken broth
2	Tablespoons lemon juice
$\frac{1}{4}$	teaspoon crushed red pepper
1	(8 ounce) frozen cooked shrimp, thawed
1	(14 ounce) can artichoke hearts, chopped
2	cups pasta, cooked
$\frac{1}{2}$	cup crumbled feta cheese

PLACE 1st 2 ingredients in bottom of crockpot.
PLACE chicken on top of onions & garlic.
COMBINE next 5 ingredients in a bowl.
MIX well. POUR over chicken. COVER.
COOK on LOW for 8 hours or HIGH for 4 hours.
STIR in shrimp & artichokes. COVER.
COOK on HIGH for 15 minutes.
SERVE over pasta. SPRINKLE with feta cheese.

Stir

To mix, usually with a spoon or fork, until ingredients are mixed together; Not to be confused with stirring up controversy. You know starting something.

GRUDGE

And when you stand praying, if you hold anything against anyone, forgive him, so that your Father in heaven may forgive you your sins.
Mark 11:25 (NIV)

BLONDE A.D.D. INTERPRETATION:

DON'T HOLD A GRUDGE
YOU WON'T BE JUDGED

YOUR INTERPRETATION:

_____ _____ _____ _____

_____ _____ _____ _____

Chicken Spaghetti Dish
"Don't Be Chicken To Forgive"

1	(8 ounce) package spaghetti noodles
4	boneless, skinless chicken breasts
2	celery stalks, chopped
1	bell pepper, chopped
½	onion, chopped
1	(4 ounce) can sliced mushrooms
1	(4 ounce) jar diced pimientos
½	cup Parmesan cheese
1½	cups cottage cheese
1	cup shredded process cheese spread
1	can cream of chicken soup
1	(14 ounce) can chicken broth
2	Tablespoons margarine, melted
½	teaspoon dried basil

COOK noodles according to directions.
BOIL chicken for 20 minutes. DRAIN. CHOP
COMBINE last 12 ingredients in a large bowl. MIX well.
POUR all ingredients in cooking sprayed crockpot. COVER.
COOK on LOW for 4 hours or HIGH for 2 hour.

SHRED

To cut or tear into long narrow strips either by hand, grater or food processor; Not to be confused with a tiny bit of evidence, or what is done to paper when you write something that is BLONDE.

COMPASSION

Be kind and compassionate to one another, forgiving each other, just as in Christ God forgave you.
Ephesians 4:32 (NIV)

BLONDE A.D.D INTERPRETATION:

FORGIVENESS... PASS IT ON YOU ARE NOT ALONE

YOUR INTERPRETATION:

_____ _____ _____ _____

_____ _____ _____ _____

PORK

BIBLE
✝

Read
with
your
♡.

READING HIS WORD

Prayer

One of the greatest treasures God ever gave the world is **His Word. The Bible. The Torah.**

Reading the Bible is like reading the recipe for How To Have A Blessed Life. It is God's recipe for living life. It is an awesome fact that the Creator of the world gave us instructions on How To Love One Another, How To Manage Our Money, How To Worship Him, How To Forgive, How To Have Peace, Joy, Hope and even How To Grieve.

God's recipe book includes historical facts that teaches us how nations have prospered when they sought the LORD and how nations have fallen when they did not seek Him. God's Word also tells us exactly what will happen in the future, prophecy. He tells us these things so we are not caught off guard, so that we will not be deceived by lies.

You may ask yourself how I know this is a good and tasty recipe. God's word says; **Oh, taste and see that the Lord is good! Blessed is the man who takes refuge in him! Psalm 34:8.**

The recipe God has given us, The Bible, has been tried and tested over thousands of years.

It is the most analyzed and scrutinized book ever written. A fake cannot stand the test of time and a bad recipe will never be cherished and passed down for generations.

Do yourself a favor and TRY God's recipe; you will want to pass this recipe down from generation to generation.

Ginger Williamson

Sweet Potatoes & Ham
"Haming Words"

3	sweet potatoes, peeled, sliced long ways
2	pounds ham, cubed
1	cup brown sugar
1	Tablespoon prepared mustard
1	(20 ounce) can pineapple chunks, with juice

PLACE potatoes in crockpot. PLACE ham over potatoes.
COMBINE last 3 ingredients in a bowl. MIX well.
POUR over ham. COVER.
COOK on LOW for 8 hours or HIGH for 4 hours.

Potatoes & Ham
"Hammed In HIS Word"

8	potatoes sliced, (leave peel on)
2	cups ham, cubed
1	onion, chopped
2	cups shredded cheddar cheese
2	cans cream of mushroom soup
	salt & pepper, to taste

LAYER all ingredients in cooking sprayed crockpot in
order given.
DO NOT MIX. COVER.
COOK on LOW for 8 hours or HIGH for 4 hours.

FOLLOW

Jesus answered, "It is written: 'Man does not live on bread alone, but on every word that comes from the mouth of God."
Matthew 4:4 (NIV)

BLONDE A.D.D. INTERPRETATION:

KNOWING GOD'S WORD HELPS US FOLLOW
LISTENING TO SATAN MAKES US HOLLOW

YOUR INTERPRETATION:

_____ _____ _____ _____ _____

_____ _____ _____ _____ _____

Cherry Pork Chops
"Cherry HIS Word"

1   (21 ounce) can cherry pie filling
4   center-cut pork chops

POUR pie filling in crockpot. ADD pork chops.
STIR to coat pork chops. COVER.
COOK on LOW for 6 hours or HIGH for 3 hours.

Italian Pork Chops
"Chop Down Satan"

2   cups Italian bread crumbs
1   cup grated Parmesan cheese
2   eggs, beaten
6   center-cut pork chops
3   Tablespoons olive oil
1   cup water

MIX 1st 2 ingredients in a bowl.
DIP pork chops in eggs.
COAT pork chops in bread crumb mixture.
BROWN pork chops in olive oil on both sides.
POUR water in crock pot.
PLACE pork chops in crockpot. COVER.
COOK on LOW for 8 hours or HIGH for 4 hours.
SERVE over pasta.

PROTECTION

Take the helmet of salvation and the sword of the Spirit, which is the word of God.
Ephesians 6:17 (NIV)

BLONDE A.D.D. INTERPRETATION:

GROW STRONG IN YOUR SALVATION THROUGH SCRIPTURE
THAT IS OUR PROTECTION FROM SATAN'S PICTURE

YOUR INTERPRETATION:

____ ____ ____ ____ ____ ____

____ ____ ____ ____ ____ ____

Pineapple Pork Chops
"Pineing HIS Word"

6   center-cut pork chops
1   (20 ounce) can pineapple chunks, with juice
½   cup brown sugar
½   cup soy sauce

COMBINE all ingredients in large zip-lock bag.
MARINATE in refrigerator overnight.
POUR all ingredients in crockpot. **COVER.**
COOK on **LOW** for 8 hours or **HIGH** for 4 hours.
SERVE over rice.

Crouton Potato Pork Chops
"HE Seasoned His Chops"

4   pork chops, ¾-inch thick
1   Tablespoon oil
     salt & pepper, to taste
3   Tablespoons margarine, melted
4   cups seasoned croutons
¾   cup water, divided
3   potatoes, peeled, quartered
2   cans cream of mushroom soup

BROWN chops in hot oil on both sides. **DRAIN.**
SPRINKLE with salt & pepper. **PLACE** in crockpot.
COMBINE next 2 ingredients with ¼ cup water.
SHAPE crouton mixture in olive-size balls.
PLACE on top of pork chops. **PLACE** potatoes in crockpot.
POUR soup over potatoes. **ADD** ½ cup water. **COVER.**
COOK on **LOW** for 8 hours or **HIGH** for 4 hours.

PORK
(Reading HIS Word)

CONVINCED

I have not departed from the commands of his lips; I have treasured the words of his mouth more than my daily bread.
Job 23:12 (NIV)

BLONDE A.D.D. INTERPRETATION:

JOB COULDN'T SENSE GOD'S PRESENCE
HE BELIEVED AND WAS CONVINCED

YOUR INTERPRETATION:

_____ _____ _____ _____ _____

_____ _____ _____ _____

Mustard Potato Pork Chops
"Knowledge Of HIS Chops"

6	pork chops, cut ¾-inch thick
2	Tablespoons oil
1	can cream of mushroom soup
¼	cup dry white wine
½	cup Dijon mustard
1	teaspoon thyme
1	garlic clove, crushed
	salt & pepper, to taste
6	potatoes, peeled, cubed
1	onion, sliced

BROWN chops in hot oil on both sides. **DRAIN.**
COMBINE remaining 9 ingredients in a bowl. **MIX** well.
POUR potato mixture in crockpot. **PUT** chops on top.
COVER. COOK on **LOW** for 8 hours or **HIGH** for 4 hours.

Rice Pork Chops
"Rice HIS Chops"

½	cup flour
2	teaspoons dry mustard
1	teaspoon garlic powder
4	center-cut pork chops
2	Tablespoons olive oil
2	cans chicken & rice soup

COMBINE 1st 3 ingredients in a bowl.
DIP pork chops in mixture. **BROWN** in oil on both sides.
PLACE pork chops in crockpot.
POUR soup over pork chops. **COVER.**
COOK on **LOW** for 8 hours or **HIGH** for 4 hours.

TEACH

But in the church I would rather speak five intelligible words to instruct others than ten thousand words in a tongue.
1 Corinthians 14:19 (NIV)

BLONDE A.D.D. INTERPRETATION:

YOU HAVE TO UNDERSTAND TO TEACH HIS COMMAND

YOUR INTERPRETATION:

_____ _____ _____ _____

_____ _____ _____ _____

Green Chilies Pork Loin
"Don't Be Green About HIS Word"

1	onion, chopped
1	(3 pound) boneless pork tenderloin, cut in cubes
1	Tablespoon oil
1	teaspoon ground cumin
1	teaspoon dried oregano
1	(14 ounce) can chicken broth
1	(4 ounce) can diced green chilies
1	(16 ounce) can stewed tomatoes
2	garlic cloves, crushed
1	teaspoon salt
1	teaspoon pepper

BROWN pork cubes & onions in hot oil in a skillet.
COMBINE all ingredients in crockpot. MIX well.
COVER. COOK on LOW for 8 hours or HIGH for 4 hours.
SERVE over rice.

French Onion Pork Loin
"Pork HIS Word"

1	(2 pound) boneless pork tenderloin
1	can cream of mushroom soup
1	can Golden mushroom soup
1	can French Onion soup

PLACE pork in cooking sprayed crockpot.
COMBINE last 3 ingredients. MIX well.
POUR over pork. COVER.
COOK on LOW for 8 hours or HIGH for 4 hours.

THOUGHT

Reflect on what I am saying, for the Lord will give you insight into all this.
2 Timothy 2:7 (NIV)

BLONDE A.D.D. INTERPRETATION:

GIVE DEEP THOUGHT
ON WHAT'S BROUGHT

YOUR INTERPRETATION:

_____ _____ _____

_____ _____ _____

Cranberry Pork Loin
"Berried With Truth"

1	(3 pound) boneless pork tenderloin
1	(16 ounce) can whole cranberry sauce
½	cup port wine
¼	cup sugar
1	lemon, thinly sliced
1	garlic clove, crushed
½	teaspoon dry mustard
1	teaspoon salt
1	teaspoon pepper
3	Tablespoons cornstarch
2	Tablespoons cold water

PLACE pork loin in crockpot.
COMBINE next 8 ingredients in a bowl. MIX well.
SPOON mixture over pork loin.
COOK on LOW for 8 hours or HIGH for 4 hours.
REMOVE pork loin from crockpot. WRAP in foil.
COMBINE water/cornstarch. STIR until smooth.
POUR in crockpot. STIR.
COOK on HIGH for 30 minutes.
STIR until thickened. SLICE pork loin.
SERVE with juices & over rice.

TRIED

"Every word of God is flawless; he is a shield to those who take refuge in him."
Proverbs 30:5 (NIV)

BLONDE A.D.D. INTERPRETATION:

TRIED AND TRUE
HE DOES RENEW

YOUR INTERPRETATION:

_____ _____ _____

_____ _____ _____

Creole Pork Loin
"Commanding Pork"

1	(2 pound) boneless pork tenderloin
½	cup flour
2	Tablespoons Creole seasoning
1	onion, chopped
1	bell pepper, chopped
2	celery stalks, sliced
2	envelopes chicken gravy mix
1	(15 ounce) can diced tomatoes, undrained

COAT pork loin in flour & Creole seasoning.
PLACE pork loin in crockpot.
PUT next 3 ingredients over pork. COVER.
COOK on LOW for 8 hours or HIGH for 4 hours.
POUR last 2 ingredients over pork loin. STIR.
COOK on HIGH for 1 hour.

Mexican Pork Loin
"Manna Loin"

1	(2 pound) boneless pork tenderloin, cubed
1	(16 ounce) jar chunky salsa
1	(14 ounce) can black beans, rinsed, drained
1	(14 ounce) can chicken broth
1	onion, chopped
1	teaspoon cumin
2	teaspoons chili powder
1	teaspoon dried oregano

COMBINE all ingredients in crockpot. MIX well. COVER.
COOK on LOW for 8 hours or HIGH for 4 hours.

COMMAND

He humbled you, causing you to hunger and then feeding you with manna, which neither you nor your fathers had known, to teach you that man does not live on bread alone but on every word that comes from the mouth of the LORD.
Deuteronomy 8:3 (NIV)

BLONDE A.D.D. INTERPRETATION:

MANNA CAME BY GOD'S COMMAND GOD'S WORD WAS THE PLAN

YOUR INTERPRETATION:

_____ _____ _____ _____ _____

_____ _____ _____ _____ _____

Roasted Pepper Tenderloin
"Roast On HIS Word"

1	(3 pound) boneless pork tenderloin
1	envelope dry ranch dressing mix
1	cup roasted red peppers
½	cup water
1	cup sour cream

PLACE pork loin in crockpot. **COMBINE** next 3 ingredients.
POUR mixture over pork. **COVER.**
COOK on **LOW** for 8 hours or **HIGH** for 4 hours.
REMOVE pork when ready to serve.
STIR sour cream into sauce in crockpot
POUR sauce over pork.

Peppercorn Pork Loin
"Corny Not To Read"

2	Tablespoons green peppercorns
3	Tablespoons sweet hot mustard
1	teaspoon horseradish
1	(3 pound) boneless pork tenderloin
1	cup apple cider
2	Tablespoons cold water
3	Tablespoons cornstarch

COMBINE 1st 3 ingredients in a bowl. **MIX** well.
SPREAD over pork. **PLACE** pork in crockpot.
POUR apple cider over pork. **COVER.**
COOK on **LOW** for 8 hours or **HIGH** for 4 hours.
REMOVE pork from crockpot. **WRAP** in foil.
COMBINE water/cornstarch. **STIR** until smooth.
POUR in crockpot. **STIR.** **COOK** on **HIGH** for 30 minutes.

PORK

(Reading HIS Word)

STUDY

Do not let this Book of the Law depart from your mouth; meditate on it day and night, so that you may be careful to do everything written in it. Then you will be prosperous and successful.
Joshua 1:8 (NIV)

BLONDE A.D.D INTERPRETATION:

STUDY OVER GOD'S WORD
THAT'S WHAT HE PREFERRED

YOUR INTERPRETATION:

_____ _____ _____ _____

_____ _____

Rosemary Potatoes & Pork Loin
"Rose Is Freed"

1   pound red potatoes, cut in fourths
1   (16 ounce) bag baby carrots
1   (3 pound) boneless pork tenderloin
3   Tablespoons Dijon mustard
2   Tablespoons dried rosemary
1   teaspoon dried thyme
        salt & pepper, to taste
1   onion, chopped
1   (14 ounce) can beef broth

ARRANGE potatoes & carrots around edge of crockpot.
PLACE pork in middle of potatoes & carrots.
COMBINE next 5 ingredients in a bowl. **POUR** over pork.
SPRINKLE onions over pork. **POUR** in broth. **COVER.**
COOK on **LOW** for 8 hours or **HIGH** for 4 hours.

Salsa Pork Loin
"Any Believer Can Salsa"

1   (2 pound) boneless pork tenderloin, 1-inch pieces
1   (20 ounce) jar chunky salsa
2   (15 ounce) cans pinto beans, rinsed, drained
        salt & pepper, to taste

PLACE pork pieces & salsa in crockpot. **MIX** well.
COVER. COOK on **LOW** for 8 hours or **HIGH** for 4 hours.
ADD last 3 ingredients to pork. **COVER.**
COOK on **HIGH** for 30 minutes. **SERVE** over cheese grits.

FREEDOM

But the man who looks intently into the perfect law that gives freedom, and continues to do this, not forgetting what he has heard, but doing it— he will be blessed in what he does.
James 1:25 (NIV)

BLONDE A.D.D. INTERPRETATION:

BELIEVER'S HEARTS ARE FREED FROM SIN WHEN THEY READ; HE COMES IN

YOUR INTERPRETATION:

_____ _____ _____ _____ _____ _____

_____ _____ _____ _____ _____ _____

Peachy Ribs
"Peachy Words"

2	pounds boneless pork ribs
¼	cup brown sugar
¼	cup ketchup
1	Tablespoon prepared mustard
1	(15 ounce) can sliced peaches, with juice

PLACE ribs in crockpot.
COMBINE last 4 ingredients. POUR mixture over ribs.
COVER. COOK on LOW for 8 hours or HIGH for 4 hours.

Sweet & Sour Ribs
"Sweet or Sour Words"

2	pounds boneless country-style pork ribs
1	teaspoon onion powder
½	teaspoon garlic power
	salt & pepper, to taste
1	cup sweet and sour sauce
1	bell pepper, cut into 1-inch pieces

PLACE ribs in crockpot. SEASON with next 4 ingredients.
COVER. COOK on LOW for 8 hours or HIGH for 4 hours.
ADD last 2 ingredients. COVER.COOK on HIGH for 2 hours.

REALISTIC

I have hidden your word in my heart that I might not sin against you.
Psalm 119:11 (NIV)

BLONDE A.D.D. INTERPRETATION:

HIS WORD WILL BECOME SIMPLISTIC SIN WON'T BE AS REALISTIC

YOUR INTERPRETATION:

_____ _____ _____ _____ _____

_____ _____ _____ _____ _____

Orange Juice Pork Roast
"Juicy Hope Roasted"

1	onion, chopped
1	(3-4 pound) pork shoulder roast
1	teaspoon salt
1	teaspoon pepper
1	(6 ounce) can frozen orange juice, thawed
$\frac{1}{4}$	cup brown sugar
$\frac{1}{2}$	teaspoon ground nutmeg
3	Tablespoons cornstarch
2	Tablespoons cold water

PLACE onion & roast in bottom of crockpot.
SPRINKLE with salt and pepper.
COMBINE next 3 ingredients. POUR over roast.
COVER. COOK on HIGH for 3 hours.
REDUCE heat to LOW. COOK for 3 hours.
REMOVE roast from crockpot. WRAP in foil.
COMBINE cornstarch/water. STIR until smooth.
POUR in crockpot. STIR. COOK on HIGH for 30 minutes.
STIR until thickened. SERVE gravy with roast & onions.

SKIM
To remove the top fat layer from stocks, soups, sauces or other liquids; Not to be confused with the way I read a book, or a kind of milk.

HOPE

For everything that was written in the past was written to teach us, so that through endurance and the encouragement of the Scriptures we might have hope.
Romans 15:4 (NIV)

BLONDE A.D.D. INTERPRETATION:

BECAUSE WE HAVE CLEAR PROMISES TO COPE
THAT'S WHY AS BELIEVERS WE HAVE HOPE

YOUR INTERPRETATION:

____ ____ ____ ____ ____ ____ ____ ____

____ ____ ____ ____ ____ ____ ____ ____

Pork Steak Dish
"You Have A Steak In Life"

1	(2 pound) pork steak, cut in strips
2	Tablespoons oil
1	onion, chopped
1	bell pepper, chopped
1	(4 ounce) can mushrooms, drained
1	(8 ounce) can tomato sauce
3	Tablespoons brown sugar
2	Tablespoons balsamic vinegar
2	teaspoons salt
2	Tablespoons Worcestershire

BROWN 1st 2 ingredients in a skillet. **DRAIN.**
COMBINE all ingredients in crockpot. **MIX** well.
COOK on **LOW** for 8 hours or **HIGH** for 4 hours.
SERVE over pasta.

Sausage & Wild Rice Dish
"Wild About Being A Nerd"

1	(16 ounce) ground sausage
3	celery stalks, chopped
1	onion, chopped
1	(6 ounce) long-grain & Wild Rice mix with seasoning
2½	cups water

BROWN 1st 3 ingredients in a skillet. **DRAIN.**
PLACE mixture in crockpot. **ADD** last 2 ingredients.
COVER. **COOK** on **LOW** for 4 hours or **HIGH** for 2 hour.

NERD

Jesus replied, "If anyone loves me, he will obey my teaching. My Father will love him, and we will come to him and make our home with him."
John 14:23 (NIV)

BLONDE A.D.D. INTERPRETATION:

OBEDIENCE IN READING HIS WORD WON'T MAKE YOU A NERD

YOUR INTERPRETATION:

_____ _____ _____ _____ _____

_____ _____ _____ _____

Read with your ♥.

Sausage Pizza
"Sausage On HIS Word"

1	(16 ounce) ground Italian sausage
1	(28 ounce) can crushed tomatoes
1	(15 ounce) can chili beans
1	(15 ounce) can black beans, rinsed
1	(2 ounce) can sliced black olives, drained
1	onion, chopped
1	bell pepper, chopped
2	garlic cloves, crushed
$\frac{1}{4}$	cup grated Parmesan cheese
1	Tablespoon dried basil
1	bay leaf
1	teaspoon salt
$\frac{1}{2}$	teaspoon sugar

BROWN sausage in a skillet. DRAIN.
COMBINE all ingredients in a crockpot. MIX well.
COVER.
COOK on LOW for 8 hours or HIGH for 4 hours.

SEASON
To enhance the flavor of foods by adding ingredients such as salt, pepper, other spices, or liquids; Not to be confused with Winter, Spring, Summer or Fall.

FOCUS

You will keep in perfect peace him whose mind is steadfast, because he trusts in you.
Isaiah 26:3 (NIV)

BLONDE A.D.D. INTERPRETATION:

READ HIS WORD; KEEP YOUR MIND FOCUSED ON HIM
YOU WILL HAVE PEACE AND BE FULL OF VIM

YOUR INTERPRETATION:

_____

_____

DESSERTS

PURPOSE

Apple Bread Pudding
"Breaded With My Name"

6   apples, peeled, seeded, cut eighths
10   slices of bread, cubed (about 4 cups)
½   teaspoon cinnamon
¼   teaspoon nutmeg
1   cup brown sugar
½   cup margarine, melted

PLACE apples in cooking sprayed crockpot.
COMBINE last 5 ingredients in a bowl. **MIX** well
POUR over apples. **COVER.**
COOK on **LOW** for 6 hours or **HIGH** for 3 hour.

Apple Butterscotch Crisp
"Buttered Up Name"

6   apples, peeled, seeded, sliced
1   cup brown sugar
½   cup all-purpose flour
½   cup quick cooking oats
1   small box butterscotch pudding mix (not instant)
1   teaspoon cinnamon
½   cup margarine, softened

PLACE apples in cooking sprayed crockpot.
COMBINE next 5 ingredients in a bowl.
CUT in margarine with fork to make crumbly.
SPRINKLE mixture over apples. **COVER.**
COOK on **LOW** for 5 hours or **HIGH** for 2 hours.

NAMED

Listen to me, you islands; hear this, you distant nations: Before I was born the LORD called me; from my birth he has made mention of my name. Isaiah 49:1 (NIV)

BLONDE A.D.D. INTERPRETATION:

GOD ALWAYS KNEW WHAT WE'D DO

YOUR INTERPRETATION:

_____   _____   _____

_____   _____   _____

Apple Peanut Butter Crumble
"Don't Crumble Your Purpose"

5	apples, peeled, seeded, sliced
$\frac{1}{2}$	cup brown sugar
$\frac{1}{2}$	cup all-purpose flour
$\frac{1}{2}$	cup quick cooking oats
$\frac{1}{2}$	teaspoon cinnamon
$\frac{1}{2}$	teaspoon nutmeg
2	Tablespoons peanut butter
$\frac{1}{4}$	cup margarine, softened

PLACE apples in bottom of crockpot.
COMBINE next 6 ingredients in a bowl. MIX well.
CUT in margarine with fork to make crumbly.
SPRINKLE mixture over apples. COVER.
COOK on LOW for 5 hours or HIGH for $2\frac{1}{2}$ hours.

Blueberry Delight
"Delight In Your Purpose"

1	(21 ounce) can blueberry pie filling
1	box yellow cake mix
$\frac{1}{2}$	cup walnuts, chopped
$\frac{1}{2}$	cup margarine, softened

PLACE pie filling in crockpot.
COMBINE next 2 ingredients in a bowl.
CUT margarine in with fork to make crumbly.
SPRINKLE mixture over pie filling. COVER.
COOK on LOW for 4 hours or HIGH for 2 hours.

PURPOSE

"Before I formed you in the womb I knew you, before you were born I set you apart; I appointed you as a prophet to the nations." Jeremiah 1:5 (NIV)

BLONDE A.D.D. INTERPRETATION:

HIS GUIDANCE WILL BECOME CLEAR WHAT YOUR PURPOSE IS HERE

YOUR INTERPRETATION:

_____ _____ _____ _____ _____

_____ _____ _____ _____

Bread Pudding
"Light Your Pudding"

5	eggs, beaten
3½	cups milk
2	teaspoons vanilla
2	Tablespoons cinnamon
6	cups bread, torn
1	cup brown sugar
1	Tablespoon margarine, melted

COMBINE all ingredients in a large bowl.
POUR mixture in cooking sprayed crockpot. COVER.
COOK on LOW for 8 hours or HIGH for 4 hours.

Raspberry Bread Pudding
"Don't Berry Your Purpose"

6	cups bread, torn
1½	cups chocolate chips
1	cup raspberries, frozen or fresh
3½	cups milk
¼	cup sugar
3	eggs, beaten

COMBINE all ingredients in a large bowl.
POUR mixture in cooking sprayed crockpot. COVER.
COOK on LOW for 8 hours or HIGH for 4 hours.

LIGHT

Your word is a lamp to my feet and a light for my path.
Psalm 119:105 (NIV)

BLONDE A.D.D. INTERPRETATION:

HIS WORD IS A LAMP TO SEE WHAT HE WANTS YOUR PURPOSE TO BE

YOUR INTERPRETATION:

___ ___ ___ ___ ___ ___ ___ ___

___ ___ ___ ___ ___ ___ ___ ___

Brownie Pudding Cake
"Prepare Your Pudding"

$\frac{1}{2}$ cup brown sugar
$\frac{3}{4}$ cup water
2   Tablespoons cocoa
$2\frac{1}{2}$ cups brownie mix (half of a box of brownie mix)
1   egg, beaten
$\frac{1}{4}$ cup peanut butter
1   Tablespoon margarine, softened
$\frac{1}{4}$ cup water
$\frac{1}{2}$ cup chocolate chips

BOIL 1st 3 ingredients in a pot.
COMBINE last 6 ingredients in a bowl. MIX well.
POUR mixture in cooking sprayed crockpot.
POUR boiled mixture over brownie mixture. COVER.
COOK on HIGH for 2 hours. TURN heat off. LET stand.

Caramel Rice Pudding
"Rice Your Purpose"

3   cups rice, cooked
2   teaspoons vanilla
1   (12 ounce) can evaporated milk
1   Tablespoon sugar
1   teaspoon cinnamon

COMBINE 1st 3 ingredients in cooking sprayed crockpot.
COVER. COOK on LOW for 3 hours or HIGH for $1\frac{1}{2}$ hours.
SPRINKLE with last 2 ingredients. STIR.

PREPARE

Trust in the LORD with all your heart and lean not on your own understanding; in all your ways acknowledge him, and he will make your paths straight.
Proverbs 3:5-6 (NIV)

BLONDE A.D.D. INTERPRETATION:

BRING YOUR DECISIONS TO GOD IN PRAYER
HE KEEPS YOUR PATH STRAIGHT TO PREPARE

YOUR INTERPRETATION:

___ ___ ___ ___ ___ ___

___ ___ ___ ___ ___ ___

Cherry Crisp
"Crispy Complete"

1	(21 ounce) can cherry pie filling
½	cup quick cooking oats
½	cup brown sugar
½	cup all-purpose flour
1	teaspoon sugar
¼	cup margarine, softened

POUR filling in cooking sprayed crockpot.
COMBINE next 4 ingredients in a bowl.
CUT margarine in with fork to make crumbly.
SPRINKLE over filling. COVER.
COOK on LOW for 5 hours or HIGH for 2 ½ hours.

Cherry Chocolate Dessert
"Cherry Me To Completion"

1	(21 ounce) can cherry pie filling
1	box chocolate cake mix
½	cup margarine, melted

POUR filling in cooking sprayed crockpot.
COMBINE last 2 ingredients in a bowl. MIX well.
SPRINKLE over filling. COVER.
COOK on LOW for 4 hours or HIGH for 2 hours.

COMPLETION

being confident of this, that he who began a good work in you will carry it on to completion until the day of Christ Jesus.
Philippians 1:6 (NIV)

BLONDE A.D.D INTERPRETATION:

GOD WILL ALWAYS COMPLETE DON'T LET SATAN DEFEAT

YOUR INTERPRETATION:

____ ____ ____ ____

____ ____ ____ ____

Chocolate Cake
"Service HIS Cake"

1	box chocolate cake mix
1	small box instant chocolate pudding
1	cup sour cream
4	eggs, beaten
$\frac{3}{4}$	cup oil
1	cup water

COMBINE all ingredients in cooking sprayed crockpot.
COVER.COOK on **LOW** for 6 hours or **HIGH** for 3 hours.

Chocolate Almond Bark Peanuts
"Don't Be A Nervous Nut"

1	(16 ounce) jar unsalted dry roasted peanuts
1	(16 ounce) jar salted dry roasted peanuts
1	(4 ounce) Bakers baking chocolate, broken
1	(12 ounce) bag chocolate chip morsels
2	pounds white almond bark, broken in pieces

POUR peanuts in crockpot. **ADD** broken chocolate.
ADD chocolate chip morsels. **ADD** almond bark.
DO NOT STIR. COVER.
COOK on **LOW** for 3 hours. **STIR** at the end of 3 hours.
DROP by teaspoonfuls on wax paper.

SERVICE

We have different gifts, according to the grace given us. If a man's gift is prophesying, let him use it in proportion to his faith.
Romans 12:6 (NIV)

BLONDE A.D.D. INTERPRETATION:

DEDICATE YOUR GIFTS TO GOD'S SERVICE GO FOR IT! DON'T BE NERVOUS

YOUR INTERPRETATION:

_____ _____ _____ _____ _____

_____ _____ _____ _____ _____

Peach Dessert
"Peachy Gifts"

2   cups frozen sliced peaches
1   Tablespoon cornstarch
½   teaspoon vanilla
¼   cup brown sugar
½   teaspoon cinnamon
1   (9 ounce) box white cake mix
4   Tablespoons margarine, melted

SPRAY crockpot with cooking spray.
LAYER all ingredients in crockpot in order given. COVER.
COOK on LOW for 6 hours or HIGH for 3 hours.

Pineapple Bake
"Baking For Your Gifts"

2   (20 ounce) cans pineapple chunks, drained
1   cup brown sugar
1   cup round buttery crackers, crushed
4   Tablespoons margarine, melted

LAYER ½ of all ingredients in order given in crockpot.
REPEAT layers. COVER.
COOK on LOW for 2 hours or HIGH for 1 hour.

GIFTS

There are different kinds of gifts, but the same Spirit. There are different kinds of service, but the same Lord. There are different kinds of working, but the same God works all of them in all men.
1 Corinthians 12: 4-7 (NIV)

BLONDE A.D.D. INTERPRETATION:

FINDING OUT OUR GIFTS GIVES US A LIFT

YOUR INTERPRETATION:

_____ _____ _____ _____

_____ _____ _____ _____

Pineapple Bread Pudding
"Bread Of Your Intentions"

1	cup margarine, softened
2	cups sugar
1	teaspoon cinnamon
4	eggs, beaten
2	(15 ounce) cans crushed pineapple, drained
5	slices of toasted bread, cut in cubes

COMBINE all ingredients in cooking sprayed crockpot.
COVER.COOK on LOW for 6 hours or HIGH for 3 hours.

Strawberry Dessert
"Berry My Intentions"

1	(21 ounce) can strawberry pie filling
1	box strawberry cake mix
½	cup margarine, softened

COMBINE 1st 2 ingredients in cooking sprayed crockpot.
CUT margarine in with fork to make crumbly.
COVER. COOK on LOW for 4 hours or HIGH for 2 hours.

TOSS
To throughly combine several ingredients by mixing lightly; Not to be confused with the act of a coin, hair or a ball.

ATTENTION

You intended to harm me, but God intended it for good to accomplish what is now being done, the saving of many lives.
Genesis 50:20 (NIV)

BLONDE A.D.D. INTERPRETATION:

GOD CAN OVERRULE OTHER'S EVIL INTENTIONS
LIVE YOUR LIFE, GET OTHER'S ATTENTION

YOUR INTERPRETATION:

____ ____ ____ ____ ____ ____

____ ____ ____ ____ ____ ____

What Do You Want To Cook?

What Do You Want To Cook?

What Do You Want To Cook?

What Do You Want To Cook?

D

DESSERTS

What Do You Want To Cook?

What Do You Want To Cook?

What Do You Want To Cook?

What Do You Want To Cook?

Perfect gift for any occasion.

Brides • Happies • Birthday • Christmas

Any Body can cook
In A crockpot
$21.95

Cooking

Reheating

Organizing

Containing

Keeping

Preparing

Observing

Timing

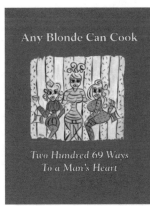

Any Blonde can cook!
$21.95

Any Blondette
can DO It!
$21.95

How to Meat a
Blonde, Brunette
or Redhead!
$21.95

See other
Products at
www.anotherblondemoment.com
601-988-1235
Order form on back

Another Blonde Moment
Order Form

Make check payable to **Another Blonde Moment** and send with
Order Form to: **P.O. Box 320747 • Flowood, MS 39232**
For more information: 601-988-1235

☐ Check or money order enclosed

Charge to: ☐ Visa   ☐ MC

Card # _____

Expiration Date _____

Signature _____

Name _____

Ship To Address _____

_____

City/State/Zip _____

_____

Phone # _____

Email Address _____

QTY.	TITLE	EACH	COST
	ANYBODY CAN COOK IN A CROCKPOT!	$21.95	
	ANY BLONDE CAN COOK!	$21.95	
	ANY BLONDETTE CAN DO IT!	$21.95	
	HOW TO "MEAT" A BLONDE BRUNETTE OR REDHEAD!	$21.95	
	SHIPPING/HANDLING	$ 7.95	
		TOTAL	

Another Blonde Moment
Order Form

Make check payable to **Another Blonde Moment** and send with
Order Form to: **P.O. Box 320747 • Flowood, MS 39232**
For more information: 601-988-1235

☐ Check or money order enclosed

Charge to: ☐ Visa   ☐ MC

Card # _____

Expiration Date _____

Signature _____

Name _____

Ship To Address _____

_____

City/State/Zip _____

_____

Phone # _____

Email Address _____

QTY.	TITLE	EACH	COST
	ANYBODY CAN COOK IN A CROCKPOT!	$21.95	
	ANY BLONDE CAN COOK!	$21.95	
	ANY BLONDETTE CAN DO IT!	$21.95	
	HOW TO "MEAT" A BLONDE BRUNETTE OR REDHEAD!	$21.95	
	SHIPPING/HANDLING	$ 7.95	
		TOTAL	